Manna in the Desert

George A. Maloney, S.J.

LIVING FLAME PRESS
BOX 74 LOCUST VALLEY, N.Y. 11560

248.3
MaM

Cover: Robert Manning

Published by:
Living Flame Press/Box 74/Locust Valley, New York 11560.

ISBN: 0-914544-54-3

Dedication

To the Brothers of St. Patrick: Edwin, Livinus and Matthew, who have opened their Novitiate and their hearts to me as a place of quiet and friendship.

Contents

Introduction

Karl Rahner, the famous Catholic theologian, once wrote that the Christian of the future would have to be a mystic or he/she would be nothing at all. The future Christian would have to experience *Someone* or he/she would hardly be able to be counted as a vibrant Christian in a post-Christian age.

Jesus Christ came among us, God in human form, to convince us, especially in His death on the cross, how madly in love His Heavenly Father is with His children. Christ died, but rose from the dead and was empowered by His Father to release His Spirit of love into our hearts (Rm 5:5). Through the infusion of the Spirit's gifts of faith, hope and love, you and I are able to experience the personalized love of God the Father, Son and Holy Spirit. This triune community of love lives within us through Baptism. It is operating at all times around us, with God's uncreated energies of love in each created atom, in each event of life.

Yet, how little of God we manage to "see" or contemplate within us and around us. What gives our lives greatest happiness and meaning is to live in love, giving and receiving love from both God and neighbor. These are the two great commandments of God.

Contemplation, the art of experiencing God through the infusion of the Spirit's gifts of faith, hope and love, should be our ordinary state of living, both on this earth and in Heaven. "And eternal life is this: to know you, the only true God, and Jesus Christ whom you have sent" (Jn 17:3). We cannot truly know, love or contemplate God without also knowing, loving and contemplating God in each other. "No one has ever seen God; but as long as we love one another God will live in us and his love will be complete in us (1 Jn 4:12).

This book, *Manna in the Desert*, is made up of various topics written to help the pilgrim-Christian progress through contemplative prayer that is very much like a journey through a desert. It is hoped that the contents of this book, when prayerfully pondered, will be as manna come down from Heaven to strengthen you in your growth in contemplative prayer.

The journey into contemplative prayer can never be merely a linear movement from one clearly marked point to another and so on to the finish line. It is a growth in love, and love is never a linear movement.

We read in the Old Testament that the Israelites wandered in the desert for forty years. They moved in circles of light, shadow and darkness. They resisted and disobeyed God. They built false idols or wanted to regress to more safe places. They learned how to find God by petitional prayer. They knew how to receive God's comforting love as they accepted their brokenness and sinfulness. They learned adoration and worship in the silence of the desert of their hearts. They were purified of self-seeking and learned to live in the essence of contemplative prayer that is total abandonment to God's will. They were sustained on their journey with mannah from Yahweh.

Jesus is the manna we receive for today's journey. His risen presence allows us to receive His indwelling presence with His Holy Spirit as the true Heavenly Manna, the Bread of life, that brings us eternal life that will never perish.

My prayer is that you, reader, will be opened to receive through these pages nourishment for your spiritual journey into deeper prayer.

These chapters originally appeared as monthly teachings I published as a newsletter called *INSCAPE*. I am grateful to *Living Flame Press* for publishing in book form the teachings that I wrote from April, 1983 through April, 1984. The ten teachings from April, 1982 through March, 1983 were also published by the same publisher in the book *Journey into Contemplation*.

George A Maloney, S.J.

St. Patrick's Novitiate
Midway City, Ca.

I

Entering the Desert

Perhaps you have expressed a desire for contemplative prayer and wish to take your first steps into a wordless type of presence before the Lord. Let us examine the signs of entrance into contemplative prayer.

Such a transition must be seen in your life of prayer as modeled on Christ's growth in prayer. St. Paul tells us that Jesus "emptied" Himself (Ph 2:7) before the Father in becoming for us a servant, obedient unto death, the death of the cross. He surrendered to the Father's Spirit at all times to allow His divinity to permeate his humanity. He was to be a revealing image of God's holiness in self-giving love through His self-sacrifice in death on the cross. Jesus had to participate and cooperate in this transforming work of the Trinity which reached its completion on the cross. There the prayer of Jesus through His active receptivity to the Father's love, would be the same as complete surrender of His total being to the Father.

So your growth in prayer is not basically a growth in any expertise as to how you are to become "centered" in God's presence or how you are to "feel" a oneness with God. It is measured by the degree of surrender in your love to God's allness. It comes about as a gift of God's immanent, indwelling presence within you to divinize and transfigure you by the Holy Spirit into a loving union of oneness. The Greek Fathers called this oneness "divinization" (*theosis*) and in Scripture it is a "participation" in God's very own nature (2 P 1:4).

Personal Cooperation

Yet you are called by God to cooperate diligently at all times to help effect this transforming union between yourself and God. Your cooperation consists in loving surrender and active receptivity to God's constant presence in your life. There is need of vigilance and inner attentiveness on your part to uproot any self-centeredness in thought, word or deed. More positively, it is to "see" God everywhere and in all things by your moving toward God as the center of all your strivings. It is to walk through this world and inwardly to be consistently one with God as He unfolds His beauty and energetic love to make all things truly work unto a harmony of good (Rm 8:28).

Father William McNamara, OCD, describes such a consistent contemplative attitude of discovering God in His inner presence found in all creatures:

> Contemplation is a pure intuition of being born of love. It is experiential awareness of reality and a way of entering into immediate communion with reality. Reality? Why, that means people, trees, lakes, mountains . . . You can study things, but unless you enter into this intuitive communion with them, you can only know *about* them, you

don't *know* them. To take a long loving look at something—a child, a glass of wine, a beautiful meal—this is a natural act of contemplation, of loving admiration . . . to be able to do that, there's the rub. All the way through school we are taught to abstract, we are not taught loving awareness.

A Growth Process

The important question we all must ask and answer is: How are we to live more consistently in truth and in love in the "real" world in which God lives as activating love? This is a process such as the human process of falling in love and growing constantly into deeper love with another. It is a slow, never-ending process. First, the seed of your union with God, and with all His creatures in love has been sown by Himself by creating you according to His own image and likeness, that is Christ (Gn 1:26). In Baptism through the Spirit's infusion of faith, hope and love the seed bursts forth into a "shoot, then the ear, the full grain in the ear" (Mk 4:27–28).

There is need on your part for a disciplined contact with God in His objective in-breaking into human history, including your present moment of personal history. This foundational prayer is called *meditation* or discursive prayer. This usually consists in taking a page from Scripture, a scene from the Old or New Testament. You go through it, reading it slowly, pondering its meaning. With your imagination, memory, understanding and will, you arrive at some affective "presence" to God. Your faith, trust and love grow slowly over months and years of such meditation. You are coming to know God in His objective reality, in His oneness through love that calls out the uniqueness of three Persons in the Trinity as the Center of all reality. That trinitarian God touches you and all creation through His two hands, as St. Irenaeus of the 2nd century writes, "Christ and the Holy Spirit."

As the Holy Spirit infuses these gifts of faith, hope and love into your heart, you are able to move from the given text to the *now* moment-presence of God and His divine action touching your life in your present history. The things, especially, that Jesus said and did, as recorded in the New Testament, become experienced by you in this moment of prayer. Jesus Christ is the same yesterday, today and always. (Heb 13:28). The *where* or the *when* are no longer so important as you enter into the process of letting go of your own control of this historical moment. This process enables you to encounter the saving Lord who transcends the limitations of all time and place through His glorious resurrectional presence living within you and in your world.

A Simplified Presence of God

As you move into this simple presence of Jesus Christ, there is a great peace and quietude. Often intense affections surge up with ardent longings to be more intimately united with Him and the Heavenly Father. The consolations in this period of your prayer life can be strong and attractive. God seems to be everywhere, even outside of your period of concentrated prayer alone with God. It is in this stage of prayer-development that many well-intended persons believe they have already entered into contemplative prayer. An evolution is taking place. A foretaste of what is to come is already yours, yet this is not contemplative prayer as your habitual framework.

As you continue to live in the global presence of Jesus Christ who surrounds you, you begin to find Him more easily in the world around you, in places and persons where you had never before "seen" Him. The lines that separated your prayer from your daily activities are beginning to fade away. You should continue to yield with greater susceptibility to His loving presence. Your aggressive activity both in prayer and in your daily actions takes on a gentleness and docility to the indwelling presence of God, both within yourself and within all of creation around you.

There is a "letting go" of your controlling power while a new sensitivity, a new listening to God's presence and loving activity around you takes over. You seem to be living on a new plateau of awareness of God's presence. Whether there are warm consolations or just dryness, filled with distractions and a seeming loss of God's presence as you formerly experienced Him, you retain a deep peace and joy that nothing can seemingly destroy or take from you.

Moving Into Contemplation

The movement from discursive prayer (which is characterized by your active control over your thoughts and affections) to enter into a more contemplative stance before God, is seen in your de-centration away from self to a surrendering to God's activity in your prayer. St. John of the Cross, the great teacher of contemplative prayer, gives us concrete signs whereby we can discern when a person moves from a discursive, meditative type of prayer into a greater simplification of faith. Here we begin the life of contemplation. It is worth quoting him in full as to these signs, in order to discern a true movement of the Spirit and a call to authentic contemplation that is quite different from tepidity and sloth in prayer:

> The first is the realization that one cannot make discursive meditation nor receive satisfaction from it as before. Dryness is now the outcome of fixing the senses upon subjects which formerly provided satisfaction. As long as one can, however, make discursive meditation and draw out satisfaction, one must not abandon this method. Meditation must only be discontinued when the soul is placed

5

in that peace and quietude to be spoken of in the third sign.

The second sign is an awareness of a disinclination to fix the imagination or sense faculties upon other particular objects, exterior or interior. I am not affirming that the imagination will cease to come and go (even in deep recollection it usually wanders freely) but that the person is disinclined to fix it purposely upon extraneous things.

The third and surest sign is that a person likes to remain alone in loving awareness of God, without particular considerations, in interior peace and quiet and repose, and without the acts and exercises (at least discursive, those in which one progresses from point to point) of the intellect, memory and will; and that he prefers to remain only in the general, loving awareness and knowledge we mentioned, without any particular knowledge or understanding.

To leave safely the state of meditation and sense and enter that of contemplation and spirit, the spiritual person must observe within himself at least these three signs together. (*The Ascent of Mount Carmel*; Bk. 2, ch. 13; Kavanaugh & Rodriguez, eds.; pp. 140–141).

Some Guidelines

As in your human friendships, so in your growing oneness with God there are some principles that need to be observed if you are to grow properly in loving union. Here are a few suggested guidelines given to help you if the Lord has led you into a more simplified form of prayer that corresponds to a movement beyond meditation or discursive prayer.

1. The most basic principle to remember is that you do not enter into contemplative prayer on any given day and remain statically fixed in a union with God that is henceforth unchanging. You do not abandon yourself completely to God in one given moment and never have a need to return to meditation or discursive thought about God. At times meditation will be possible and even desirable. At other times reading a few prayers may be helpful at the beginning of prayer to localize yourself before God's awesome presence. The use of the Jesus Prayer can be an excellent means of centering yourself deeply in the presence of the Trinity and thus putting yourself deeply into a more "faith-full" presence of God.

2. The mere emptying of your mind of any discursive movement of thoughts and maintaining a state of inner "void" cannot always be construed automatically as a superior state of contemplative prayer. Thomas Merton warns against such a "vacuity" which can all too often be a psychological withdrawal from reality if this is merely self-induced and not coming from a leading of the Holy Spirit. He writes: "One who does this of set purpose . . . simply enters into an artificial darkness of his own making. He is not alone with God, but alone with himself. He is not in the presence of the Transcendent One, but of an idol: his own complacent identity. He becomes immersed and lost in himself, in a state of inert, primitve and infantile narcissism" (*Contemplative Prayer*: p. 90)

3. The true test of whether you are removing the crutches of images and ideas and your own wordy speeches to the Lord in prayer and are going deeper into the darkness of faith and meeting the living God is to be seen in your living the difference between *obscurity* and *vagueness*. From the psychological aspect, both conditions of emptying your mind from thoughts and your own discursive powers seemingly are the same, namely, you are emptied and you are passive. *Vagueness* is such emptiness that shows itself throughout the day in your heart that is not emptied, however, of self. There is no searching humbly to surrender each

thought, word and deed to the dominion of God. This is rooted in an emptiness that is filled with the false ego.

Obscurity is the condition of true pilgrims moving into deeper contemplation. It is an emptiness of everything in order that in inner poverty you can stretch out in the desert of your creatureliness and inner dread to cry continually to see the face of the Lord. It is the virgin in all of us who surrenders to the allness of God: "Be it done unto me according to Thy word."

4. The best test of whether you are sincerely seeking God's glory in true contemplative prayer and not feeding your own false ego in such prayer is the actuality of your life. As you pray, so you live. If your aloneness with the Alone and the total stripping of yourself of any independence away from God is authentic and truly contemplative, it will show itself in greater love toward your neighbor, the litmus test of true union and self-surrender to God. This will require an intensification of your self-reflection on the quality of your daily living. Check any sinful attachment or imperfections that might be at the root of such dryness or seeming separation from God's presence. Abandonment to God in contemplation avoids the errors of Quietism that so sickly gave up all activity on the part of the contemplative, especially in the area of self-examination and inner attentiveness throughout the day.

5. You may be tempted to doubt that your more simplified prayer is really prayer pleasing to God, and, because of distractions and dryness, you may wish to return to a former level of discursive prayer. Your activity should now consist mainly in gently pushing your will to become more united with that of God, even though there may be extreme dryness and even harmless distractions that cannot be avoided. It is to be expected that, as you stop using your discursive powers of intellect, will and imagination, there will be much wandering of these faculties in search of images and ideas upon which to feed.

In the first stages of contemplation, the prayer of faith, a definite purgation process takes place with the slowing down of the use of faculties you so long used in praying to God. Even though the thought of God does not necessarily bring any consolation, your faith is being exercised in a new way, freed from any ideas or words. St. John of the Cross describes what is taking place in such contemplative prayer without words or images: "Since God puts a soul in this dark night in order to dry up and purge its sensory appetite, He does not allow it to find sweetness or delight in anything" (*The Dark Night*, p. 313).

6. Learn to grow through the tribulations you experience in such prayer. You are being called by God to acquire humility by forsaking all your own self-possession and to abandon yourself totally to God's freedom to come to you as He wishes, when He wishes. Without trials be assured there is no humility. Only in such inner poverty will you be capable of receiving God's mercy and experience your regeneration as a child of God, through the infusion of the Holy Spirit.

If you are blessed to have a soul-friend to accompany you on your desert journey into contemplation, he/she will hopefully know from personal experience and the tradition of Christian mystics down through the ages, the value of such trials. He/she will not encourage you to return to a former level of prayer only to avoid greater conflict and, therefore, to turn away from God's call to enter into a sharing in the death-resurrection of Christ.

7. Perhaps the greatest obstacle you will face in the beginning stages of contemplative prayer will be discouragement. This can take many forms and can be the result of many problem areas of your prayer life. You can readily understand why you must be constantly on your guard to fight discouragement in prayer, since you are dealing with a relationship between yourself and God that unfolds in an ever-increasing atmosphere of dark faith.

This type of rarefied existence is hardly "natural" to you. You and I are born with a propensity to take charge of our lives, to make decisions with ourselves as the center of focus. To go to prayer daily and seek constantly throughout your daily life to surrender in faith to the loving presence of God whom you cannot see with your senses or "feel" any more by consoling affections is a wearing process. It tears down your body and brings discouragement to your mind.

Even when you honestly and sincerely are trying to grow in prayer and to cooperate with the movements of the Holy Spirit, there will be great discouragement as you move away from your active control of things in prayer to surrender to the activity of God.

But discouragement often can come from lack of inner discipline, from sloth, from self-centeredness, all of which, in the beginning stages of contemplative prayer seek things such as consolations and insights from God. One wants to "feel" the love of God as God was experienced in a lower level of affectionate prayer. Little by little you may slack off in your efforts to prepare yourself for your daily encounter with the living God of Abraham, Isaac and Jacob. With little "success," judged from your own criteria, you may fall victim to discouragement and often cut down on your prayer, if you do not give it up completely.

Also, as we become very anxious in our prayer, activism and our great desire to succeed in our daily work bring us into a discouragement. Physical and mental fatigue exhaust us. Such discouraging elements set the stage for many distractions. Here is when we must learn to abandon our work and even the degree of "worldly" success to God as we strive to live in true humility.

Death Unto Life

Ultimately true contemplation is complete surrender to God's love that directs you at every step of your life. It is an ongoing process that knows no end. But it evolves into a transfiguring union with God and a loving oneness between you and your neighbor and all of God's creatures. You attain this union and oneness through the purification of your self-centeredness in order to enter into the transformation into Christ. It is a risk to let go of discursive prayer when God is calling you to greater union with Him. But there is no other way to become holy and a true Christ as St. Paul discovered: "I have been crucified with Christ, and I live now not with my own life but with the life of Christ who lives in me. The life I now live in this body I live in faith: faith in the Son of God who loved me and who sacrificed himself for my sake" (Gal 2:20–21).

This is to seriously live our Baptism into the trinitarian life in which God, Father, Son and Holy Spirit become at each moment our complete *All*. Hugh of St. Victor has well described this state of union with God where God comes and goes, yet always remains. Only He is loved truly by the Christian:

> Yes, it is truly the Beloved who visits thee. But He comes invisible, hidden, incomprehensible. He comes to touch thee, not to be seen; to intimate His presence to thee, not to be understood; to make thee taste of Him, not to pour Himself out in His entirety; to draw thy affection, not to satisfy thy desire; to bestow the first-fruits of His love, not to communicate it in its fullness. Behold in this the most certain pledge of thy future marriage: that thou art destined to see Him and to possess Him eternally, because He already gives Himself to thee at times to taste; with what sweetness thou knowest. Therefore, in the times of His absence thou shalt console thyself; and during His visits thou shalt renew thy courage which is ever in need of heartening. We have spoken at great length, O my soul, I ask thee to think of none but Him, love none but Him, listen to none but Him, to take hold of none but Him, possess none but Him.

II

Desert Silence

There can be no true growth in deeper prayer and union with God without silence on all levels of our being: physical, psychic and spiritual. Silence, especially on the spiritual level, becomes the inner poverty of spirit which Jesus called blessed, for to such the Kingdom of God would be given (Mt 5:3). It is nothing less than living in the habitual state of truth we call *humility*. The Spirit reveals to us in the emptying of all our control over God and the way we want our lives to go, how we should live in the allness of God. We then reach the fullness of our true selves in His love.

Karl Rahner describes what happens when we become silent:
If we are silent, if we forgive, if without reward we give ourselves wholeheartedly and are detached from ourselves, we are reaching out into a limitlessness which exceeds any assignable bound and

which is nameless. We are reaching out towards the holy mystery which pervades and is the ground of our life. We are dealing with God.

God speaks His Word that is light, revelation, speech and meaning to those who attune themselves to His silent speaking of that Word. We are to wait in "aweful" expectancy for God's gratuitous gift of His Word spoken when we surrender ourselves to His mysterious gift of love. To understand this basic paradox of hearing God in silence, of seeing Him by not seeing, is to understand our movement in relation to God as a transition from knowledge to love.

For you to turn within and accept the silence surrounding you as remote yet present, to accept your humility and poverty as part of your true existential being, to accept God's presence as loving and healing, is to live in faith. It is in the silenced heart that you learn to know God is God and you learn to love Him as your Father.

Silence and Contemplation

True contemplation is ultimately listening in surrendering love to God's Word. This word speaks from within the depths of our being and in the context of our daily lives. But there can be no true listening in love without deep silence. One of the most needed commodities in our modern life is silence. Yet you cannot buy it. It is true that the wealthy can afford to buy seclusion from the crowds on their private estates, away from inner city noise and dirt. But silence is more than the mere absence of noise.

Have you ever found yourself in a still forest where the only noise came from the breeze blowing through the pine trees or from an occasional bird call? Yet inside yourself there may have been much noise. Mentally you were wrestling with a problem and you did not enjoy inner peace. You may also have experienced an inner quiet amidst much external noise, such as riding the subway or on an airplane. This silence was like a calming, creative force flowing over you from within. It is this type of silence that is so desperately needed in our world today.

The poet Longfellow expressed this inner silence as an inward stillness:

> Let us, then, labor for an inward stillness-
> An inward stillness and an inward healing;
> That perfect silence where the lips and heart
> Are still, and we no longer entertain
> Our own imperfect thoughts and vain opinions,
> But alone speaks in us, and we wait
> In singleness of heart, that we may know
> His will, and in silence of our spirits,
> That we may do His will, and do that only.

Afraid to be Alone

To enter into your inner being, you must embrace silence. Yet this is a discipline that we find most difficult to embrace. We find ourselves resisting this at every turn. We will do almost anything to "remain up" on surface, in command of our lives by means of our discursive powers. Given any situation, we have the power to fashion it by our minds according to our own liking. We can truly create our own world. Many times we mistakenly call this our "creative" power!

In reality, such power can be our undoing deterring the healing process by which we become a wholly integrated person, the person God knows us to be, when from the depths of our being He calls us by our name (Is 43:1). We are masters at avoiding confrontation with our real person. We can play games, put on masks and become distracted by the words and values that people around us live by. We can busy ourselves "saying" prayers or even in so-called "silent" prayer we can refuse to enter into a real silence to look at our inner feelings. We do not look at both the light and the darkness that are struggling for possession of us. As long as we indulge in such game-playing it means we are afraid to be silent and alone with God. We fear to look inwardly and honestly ask for healing from the Transcendent God when we see, through genuine self-knowledge, what needs to be sacrificed and transformed.

Dr. Carl G. Jung describes the difficulty entailed in becoming self-recollected because we fear living more consciously:

> To make a sacrifice is an act of self recollection, a gathering together of what is scattered, — the things in us that have never been properly related, and a coming to terms with oneself with a view of achieving full consciousness.
>
> Self-recollection is about the hardest and most repellent thing there is for man, who is predominantly unconscious. Human nature has an invincible dread of becoming more conscious of itself. Nobody can give what he has not got. So anyone who can sacrifice himself and forego his claim, must have had it, i.e., that he must have knowledge of the claim.
>
> To sacrifice proves that you possess yourself for it does not mean just letting yourself be passively taken. It is a conscious and deliberate self-surrender, which proves you have control of yourself, of your ego.

The Silence of God

To understand the creative power in silence, we must understand something about God's own silence. Today some theologians, taking their cue from in-depth psychiatry, speak not only about the light of God, but also about the darkness in Him. At the basis of creativity, the bringing of something into being out of nothingness or out of chaos, there must be a confrontation of the indeterminate, the realm of darkness.

St. John's first epistle describes God as light and in Him there is no darkness. Yet St. John continually in that same epistle tells us that God is love. God is love and silence is the perfect communication of the Father and His Son through the Holy Spirit. There is a necessary *kenotic* (emptying) element in any love relationship. This word "kenosis", used by St. Paul, means that God goes out toward His Son, pouring all that He is into His Son. "Jesus Christ *emptied* Himself, becoming man and obedient unto death, the death of the cross." (Phil. 2:6)

God needs no multiplicity and variety to express His eternal continuity in love. He loves and pours Himself completely out into His one Word and this one Word receives the fullness of the Father in the silence of one Word. St. Paul writes: "In him lives the fullness of divinity" (Col 2:9).

God not only speaks His Word in silence from all eternity without any interruption but He also hears this word in perfect silence as an echo of his own reflected beauty and love. Through the silent gasp of love that is the Holy Spirit bringing God the Father together with His Son, the Heavenly Father hears His Word continually coming back to Him. The word returns in a perfect, eternal "yes" of total, surrendering Love that is again the Holy Spirit.

God's Creative Silence in Nature

Through God's one Word, as St. John writes in his prologue, all of creation is brought forth into existence. Mountains and oceans, birds and beasts, flowers and grains tumble forth in profuse richness from the finger tips of the creating God—and all is done in silence! When we can withdraw from our busy, fragmented worlds that pull us in so many directions, filling us with frustrations and anxieties, and enter into God's silence found in all primeval nature, then we are opening ourselves up to deep healing. When you enter into the primeval, endless *now* of God's quiet, you enter into a stage of *being*. It is hardly a state of passivity or idleness. It is beyond pragmatic descriptions. It is where life and love merge into the same experience.

If we wish to encounter God on a deeper level of communication than that of concepts, we must learn how to enter into the restful silence of God. We must learn to draw upon the richness of solitude that the physical world has to offer us. It was at such a time that Pascal cried out: "The eternal silence of those boundless spaces strikes awe into my soul." At such times when we begin to hear God's love and beauty pouring forth in His silence throughout all of nature, we can pray with St. Augustine:

> Heaven and earth and all that is in the universe cry out to me from all directions that I, O God, must love Thee, and they do not cease to cry out to all so that they have no excuse.

God's energies pulsate in all of the animate nature of plants, trees, birds and animals, that cry out unceasingly to us noisy pilgrims along life's highways," . . . . in Him we live and move and have our being" (Ac 17:28). When we become silent we discover that God is our God as the Psalmist says (Ps 47:10). God works efficiently throughout all of nature and He accomplishes His purpose in silence. How silently the butterfly moves about, telling us of God who loves us in silence! How quietly the giant sequoia has been growing for centuries as it stretches its head toward its Maker in silent praise and admiration!

When I find my life becoming filled with much chaotic movement and noise, I slip back to a farm in Georgia where I once spent three months in prayer and writing. In the evening it was so soothing and healing to sit by the lake and watch the sun go down upon the quiet waters. Night brought peace and rest to all of nature and to my inner self as well. I and all of nature were one in the Source of our common Creator. In the early morning hope was vividly experienced in the flaming colors spangling the scattered clouds of the sky. The birds seemed to be shouting to the world to wake up and come alive and be filled with hopeful joy.

Such moments may be infrequent for city dwellers, yet we must find ways to "come apart and rest awhile" as Jesus invited his disciples (Mk 6:31). Only in peaceful quietness can we first become consciously aware of God's presence and then sincerely let Him speak to us.

Even though moments of escape into primeval nature may be rare in our urban living, nevertheless, we need to learn how to turn into our "hearts" and find God breathing forth His healing love in silence.

A Silenced Heart

We of all God's creations have been made "according to God's image and likeness" (Gn 1:26). Deep down at the core of your innermost being is found the focal point that Holy Scripture calls your heart. It was here that Jesus told us to pray to our Heavenly Father.

> But when you pray, go to your private room and, when you have shut your door, pray to your Father who is in that secret place and your Father who sees all that is done in secret will reward you (Mt 6:6).

Bossuet in a moving sermon shows that man's greatest dignity consists in having a soul that is the breath of God, the sigh of God's heart. The Holy Spirit, is breathed into man to make for him a uniquely living spirit-to-Spirit relationship. "Our soul is also a breath, a sigh from the heart of

19

God and in it God takes great pleasure outside of Himself."

God's silence grows deeper and more intense when He communicates with you than in His activity in other creatures. As he gives Himself more directly to you in the depths of your being, in your heart, God does so in the silence of begetting His Word through the fiery gaze of the Spirit of Love. But what a struggle for us to become silent before God's silent love! It entails a letting go of the control that we have over our lives. It necessitates a death to our false selves in order to find our true selves in the Other, dwelling intimately within us.

Nikos Kazantzakis describes this decision to yield to God: "God is a fire and you must walk on it . . . dance on it. At that moment the fire will become cool water. But until you reach that point, what a struggle, my Lord, what agony!"

It is the struggle to enter into the darkness of faith and there to accept the silent love of the indwelling Trinity. St. Augustine exhorts us: "Enter into yourself; it is in the interior man where Truth is found." When we have the courage to drop our defenses and sink into the inner darkness, we enter into a new experience of knowing by not knowing. After some experience of praying in silence without words and masks, we learn to let go. We breathe psychologically more deeply, more peacefully. It seems that we have been given new, interior eyes that lovingly gaze on Him. In this silent gaze we know ourselves in God's unique love for us. With new interior ears we ever so quietly listen to God as He communicates Himself to us without words, images or forms.

Our prayer in such silence through the deepening of faith infused into us by the Holy Spirit brings with it a great peace because we are touching God who resides at the center of our being. Our prayer now is not something that we do so much as an entering into a state of being. It is an *enstasis*, a standing inside, to best describe the prayer of the heart that unfolds in deep, interior silence. I stand in God, in His holy presence, loving Him without words or images. Yet the totality of my being is in a tranquil state of loving surrender.

Silence—A Continued Process of Growth

Silence admits of many degrees. There can be a physical silence exterior to ourselves. There can be a physical silence within our members: stillness of the limbs, the absence of speech. There can be various degrees of psychic silence of the emotions, the imagination, the memory, the intellect and the will. But the greatest silence is that of our spirit communing with God's Spirit. "Heart speaks to heart" in silence that is the language of self-surrendering love.

This is a state of highest expanded consciousness brought about by an increased infusion of faith, hope and love by the Holy Spirit. It is only the Holy Spirit who assures us that we are united with God and truly growing in greater loving union. It is also the Holy Spirit who brings forth His gifts and fruits in our relationships toward others. Our lives, now rooted more deeply in the ultimate, reflect more exactly than at any other earlier stage, the worth of our prayer-life.

Such silence in our spirit is a gift of God's Spirit of love. The Holy Spirit dwelling within us teaches us how to pray deeply in the heart ". . . . the love of God has been poured into our hearts by the Holy Spirit who has been given us" (Rm 5:5). It is God "who gives you His Holy Spirit" (1 Th 4:8). Our bodies through Jesus Christ have become temples of the Holy Spirit (1 Co 6:19).

We are utterly incapable of praying in silence to God as we should. Such silence is a continued process of letting go and allowing the Holy Spirit to pray within us. "For when we cannot choose words in order to pray properly, the Spirit Himself expresses our plea in a way that could never be put into words . . ." (Rm 8:26–27).

It is the Spirit that gives life (Jn 6:63). The redemptive work of Christ can be seen as a continued process taking place in the silence of our hearts in deep prayer. He is releasing the Spirit within us as He had promised He would (Lk 11:13). The Spirit allows us to transcend the limitations of words and ideas about God in order to enter into the silent langauge of love. It is an experience that transcends anything controllable or wrought by our human powers. The Spirit of Jesus sent into our hearts allows us to know His presence and to yield to His love toward the Father and the Son (Jn 14:17).

Freedom in the Spirit

This Spirit "reaches the depths of everything, even the depths of God" (1 Co 2:10). It is thus that we are taught by God's very own Spirit of love, making us "spiritual" beings. If in deep, silent prayer you are to touch the very depths of God, this can be done only through His Spirit. ". . . in the same way the depths of God can only be known by the Spirit of God. Now instead of the spirit of the world, we have received the Spirit that comes from God, to teach us to understand the gifts that He has given us. Therefore we teach . . . in the way that the Spirit teaches us; we teach spiritual things spiritually" (1 Co 2:11–13).

To contemplate is to move beyond our own activity to be activated by the inner power of the Holy Spirit. It means to be swept up into the triadic love current of Father, Son and Holy Spirit. In the silent prayer of the heart, a gift of the Spirit praying within us, we move beyond feelings, emotions, even thoughts. The Spirit is so powerfully operative that we feel any activity of ours through imaging or reasoning can only be noise that disturbs the silent communication of God at the core of our being.

If I introduce noise by speaking words and fashioning images of God, then I am limiting His freedom to speak His Word as He wishes, when He wishes. When we are in deep silence and humble self-surrender, the Holy Spirit frees us so God can give Himself to us with utter freedom and joy.

Silence—The Language of the Innermost Self

By plunging down into our innermost self in silence we

make contact with God as healer. As long as we live superficially, noisily dispersed amidst a world of ever-mounting
multiplicity with its accompanying meaninglessness, we will
not know the health of body, soul and spirit that God wishes
us to enjoy.

Inner health comes through the silencing of our own im-
pulsiveness toward dispersion. Like Mary, the Mother of
God, who opened herself in the Annunciation so totally to
the Holy Spirit, as St. Luke records in his first chapter, we
too allow that Word of God to be born within the depths of
our being. Our "heart," the core of our being, becomes a
womb that in silence and darkness receives God's Word. The
Heavenly Father brings forth His Word within us, ever so
gently, ever so gradually.

The central teaching of Christianity is that God by grace,
His uncreated energies, is present within us. But how few of
us desire to live in the silence that is the environment and the
language in which this communication with God's life takes
place! We lack the discipline and patience needed to culti-
vate the presence of God through the inward journey. The
whole realm of asceticism, of bringing our passionate nature
under submission to the delicate movements of the Spirit,
assumes an importance as a preparation necessary if our
spirit is to be brought into perfect accord with God's Spirit.

Prayer is listening, it is yielding to the Word of God that
is being spoken constantly by the indwelling Father through
His Spirit. And silence is the langauge of this communication. Another word for this inner silence is "recollection." It
means to be pulled together from our habitual dispersion to
reach a "still point" of attentiveness in order that God may
speak to us as He wishes.

The person of deep prayer learns to live in this silent
recollection, a focussing in upon God as the inner center of
one's being. The gap of separateness keeping us from greater
union with God can be bridged if we conquer the noise of
our own state of limited consciousness. We control our lives
to let God become the guide of our lives in the silence of our
weakened condition.

Having reached this state of interior silence and recollection, we are gifted by God's Spirit with a kind of knowledge of God that ordinary consciousness could never provide. The struggling and searching blindly in darkness give way to a "hearing" in silence, a seeing "with a loving, striving, blindly beholding the naked being only of God Himself" (*The Cloud of Unknowing*).

Silence is the language of deeper, infused prayer that the Holy Spirit gives to God's poor children who hunger and thirst for His Word. It ultimately is the ability to live in mystery. For those who enter into this mystery, there is real communication, deep love, full healing and maturity. But few are ready to pay the price to enter deeply into mystery and stay there. Jesus, not Moses, is waking you up from your sleep and asking you whether you want to leave Egypt. But you must cross over the Red Sea and live in the desert for a long time. Are you willing?

III

He Has Pitched His Tent Among Us

The liturgical Feast of the Nativity celebrates God's infinite emptying of Himself in the incarnation of His only begotten Son, Jesus Christ (Ph 2:10) and our infinite enrichment in that love to become participators in His very own divine nature (2 Pet 1:4). God gives us His perfect gift, His Son, not only as a present, but according to the root meaning of the word, present, as His everlasting, intimate *presence* among us. God's mystery of divine love is that He desires to give Himself to us human beings in an immanent, indwelling presence. His presence is built upon the elements of true, intimate presence: total *availability*, *mutuality* of two becoming one in a union of love that results in a continued *interchange* of God's triune community of Father, Son and Holy Spirit as gift to us.

The Good News

The Good News of Christianity is God's revelation that God calls us to intimacy. We can live for and with other human persons. But God's infinite goodness and love call us to share His happiness by living in Him. God's awesome transcendence, Christianity teaches, paradoxically makes Him *immanently* present within us in an incomprehensible but total way of self-giving to us.

God's uncreated energies of love penetrate every part of our being. They invade us most intimately so that in Him we live and move and have our being (Ac 17:28). God, as a triune community of Father, Son and Holy Spirit, lives within us in our deepest consciousness level that Scripture calls our *heart*. But the Good News is that God so loves us that we can, through His incarnated Word, Jesus Christ, become totally transformed into Him.

God Among Us

The incarnation makes it possible for God in His Word to "pitch His tent" and dwell among us. The Good News coming from the birth of Christ is that this all-loving God is not far from us. Although there will always remain something unapproachable, unpossessable and unfathomable about God, the Trinity, yet Jesus Christ's role in His incarnation, death, resurrection is to pour the love of God into our hearts (Rm 5:5). He has given His Spirit to us so that we can "know" and experience God as a community of loving persons.

This reality is the end of the incarnation, death and resurrection of Jesus Christ. He came among us to make it possible, not only that we might become children of God but that at all times we might live in that continued awareness discovered in each moment of our lives. This is your dignity: to be called children of God and you really are such (1 Jn 3:1) in the process of discovering and surrendering to the un-created energies of God living within you and within the context of each human situation or event. God is saying in substance to you in each moment: "Here I am; experience my love. This place is holy. Take off your shoes, your securities, and approach this burning bush to become consumed by the fire of My divine love for you."

Contemplative Knowledge

This highest union, the infused union of the Trinity, in which God communicates Himself as Father, Son and Spirit, is not achieved by any conceptual knowledge but through an immediate, experiential knowledge wherein He opens Him-self to you.

You can never come to this knowledge through your own concepts or thinking process. God, purely and simply, in His transcendence, reveals Himself to you when He wishes and as He wishes. It is not so much that God does something new and different to you after years of your own preparation and cooperation through continued purification of your heart from self-centeredness. He is always present, the same lov-ing Father, Son and Spirit, loving you with an infinite, un-created love.

But when you have cracked open the door of your heart and you finally open it, you stand before what was always there. "Behold I stand at the door and I knock. He who opens, I will enter and sup with him" (Rv 3:20). In a state of humility you break yourself of your own power to possess your life, to take love and to control both God and others. Then you enter into the reality that was always there. With Moses we have to climb up the mountain to reach God by a knowing that is an unknowing, a darkness that is truly lu-minous. As you separate yourself from all limitations you place on God and from all attachments to your own self-love, you reach the top of the mountain.

There in the darkness of the storming clouds you hear the notes of the trumpet and you see those lights that no human method could ever give you. No human mind, no guru, no technique could ever bring you God's personalized gift of Himself. God has to take over the communication of Himself to you directly. No one but God can give Himself to you. God so loves you as to give you His Son so that in believing in Him you might live forever (Jn 3:16). His Son is sheer gift, but the good news is that the gift is God Himself!

This is the awesome mystery of the good news: that we can experience God sharing with us His very own being and divinizing us into His own children. "Think of the love that the Father has lavished on us, by letting us be called God's children; and that is what we are . . . My dear people, we are already the children of God but what we are to be in the future has not yet been revealed; all we know is, that when it is revealed we shall be like him because we shall see him as he really is" (1 Jn 3:1–2).

Living in God's Presence

For true Christians who are moving into true contemplation of the key mysteries of their faith, the birth of Christ is every day, is happening at this moment. God's love in Christ Jesus through His Spirit is being incarnated in this concrete moment in your living situation. Contemplation is the God-given gift through the Spirit's infusion of faith, hope and love that you might enter into the *kairos*, the moment of salvation of God's healing love for you. It is not only to remember the historical moment of what happened in a cave near Bethlehem centuries ago as Mary gave birth to her Son, but it is to experience the birth of Christ, of God-Man, now happening in your place in history but also happening in God's eternal *now* moment.

Your goal in life is to convert your life at every moment into a loving response, as you continually experience in deepening consciousness the infinite love of God for you. In the birthing of Christ in your heart, God's choicest and most perfect gift of loving presence is given to you. Your response is to live at each moment in an exchange of a loving gift of yourself to God. You are being birthed also into your true being in Christ as you exchange the gift of yourself by becoming a loving presence to Him in this moment that leads you into the next moment.

You want to move your will so that at each moment you wish to surrender yourself in total gift back to God. This can be done only to the degree that you experience God's great love for you in this moment. God is completely and totally present to you in His self-giving. God, Father, Son and Holy Spirit, cannot be more present or more self-giving than He is to you in this moment. The question is: How can you become more present to Him? How can you become total gift to God?

To give, not things, but ultimately oneself, is the essence of love. Love lavishes goods, gives all without reserve if the love that you receive is consciously experienced from God as a similar love without reserve. Love begets the same kind of love experienced. How can you continue ever more to experience this infinite love? How can you hold yourself in the state of oneness, your will attached solely at all times to the will of God? This is God's gift through His Spirit of Christ. It comes through infused faith, hope and love.

Yet you can cooperate to dispose yourself for this increased gift of awareness of God's intimate, loving presence in each moment. No one but yourself can raise your mind and heart toward God and gift God with the free gift of yourself. But this gifting of yourself to God takes place in the context of your every moment, in the deeds, words and thoughts that you permeate with your self-giving love to God.

Aloneness with the Alone

Many Christians would like to live each moment contemplating God's presence as love and surrendering themselves in love back to God. But how few Christians are ready to be alone with the Alone before they seek to find God in the many? Jesus teaches us to go out as He did to preach and to be a healing love to the broken ones of our world. But He also shows us that before He went out among people as the Divine Physician, he had continued need to go aside and to be alone with His Heavenly Father in experienced exchange of gifts of each other. We read in the Gospel: "He would always go off to some place where he could be alone and pray" (Lk 5:16).

At times this was to go out into a deserted place; at other times it was to go up the mountain to find His aloneness with the Alone. In such moments of "birthing" in which He was becoming His true self in the Father's love through the Spirit poured into His heart, Jesus emptied Himself as total gift to the Father. His giving in loving service to other human beings who came into His daily life, was in proportion to the experienced love the Father revealed He had for His Son.

Husbands and wives need aloneness with each other to give them an awareness of their beauty through the exchange of the gift of each other. You and I have continued need for times to be alone with God, our Bridegroom, as Jesus so often revealed to us on the pages of the New Testament. The being alone with God in "aloneness" prayer, should never be an occasion to separate yourself from your love and service to others. Certainly it should never be a source of feeding one's false ego in self-seeking, rather than in true *kenotic* living for God in self-surrendering Christmas love.

In the Still of the Night

It was in the still of the night that angels announced the Birth of the Christ to poor, humble shepherds who were watching their flock near Bethlehem. It is in the silence within our hearts that Jesus is birthed into new life. He truly abides

with His Father and His Spirit within our deeper consciousness. God gives Himself to us directly, beyond all concepts,
images and even feelings. In the depths of our beings, our
hearts are the birthing stable where the Christ Child is again
born on this earth. God gives us Himself in the silence of His
begetting His Word through the fiery gaze of the Spirit of
love.

But what a struggle most of us undergo to become silent
before God's silent love! It means first of all that we discipline ourselves to meet our living God, Father, Son and Holy
Spirit, in an aloneness that admits of a physical silence. We
are taken away from the multiplicity of activities and noises
around us, to return to that primal silence in which God is
always speaking to all creation in His Word. Do you have a
time each day when you can be alone with God? True Christian contemplation, the finding of God in all things, cannot
happen unless you can find God dwelling within your very
being, in your heart.

It is in such physical silence that a greater surrender of
yourself to God's movements in prayer can unfold on higher
levels of psychic and spiritual silence. As you relax in the
physical silence both around you and within your body, you
breathe more deeply, more peacefully. You begin to go down
with greater ease into your inner self and joyfully stretch out
your spiritual hands. You grasp God who now is so close to
you in your consciousness through surrender of yourself to
God's movements in faith, hope and love. In such faith you
know that you are touchng God who resides at the center of
your being. Your prayer now is not something that you *do*,
so much as an entering into a state of *being*. You seem to be
standing inside your real self, not outside. Inside your deepest reality you are truly centered *in* God. You stand in His
holy presence, loving Him without words or images or
props. The totality of your being is in a tranquil state of loving surrender.

Such integrated silence permeating your body, soul and
spirit relationships before God can bring about complete listening with utter sincerity and honesty in the depths of your

being. It requires a certain amount of time. Persons, serious about contemplative prayer, busy people in a family situation, called to a job outside the home or community, often ask, "How long a time should I give to my individual prayer before God? How can loving communion be cajoled into a time slot?"

We all know that such integration of body, soul and spirit into a total person, dynamically aware of the gift of the other, does take a certain amount of time. From my own experience in directing many contemplative people, I would hold that an hour would not be too minimal to be alone with God. I personally have found it better for me to divide such an hour into a half hour during the middle of the night and another half hour upon rising. Others might find it better to devote an intense half hour of deep communion with the triune God in the early morning and another half hour before the evening meal.

Living in God's Presence

You cannot remain in such aloneness with God if you are also listening to God's call to go forth and witness to what you have experienced. The shepherds ran in haste to find in the stillness of a cave, the newborn Savior, a Babe in the manger. They had need to go forth from that experience and share it with others. We read: "And the shepherds went back glorifying and praising God for all they had heard and seen; it was exactly as they had been told" (Lk 2:20).

Is this not similar to ourselves in prayer? We contemplate the mysteries that the Church holds out to us so that we may experience exactly as we have been told. We encounter the good news in Christ Jesus and to that degree we go forth to glorify and praise God by the lives we live in that experienced oneness with Christ.

You can change your life gradually by pushing yourself gently under the power and movement of the Spirit of love, to align yourself in all your being with the being of God as self-giving love. You wish to do all to please God. You desire to have no desire but to glorify God. He becomes your "magnificent obsession." Every thought, word and deed becomes motivated by the desire to love God with your whole heart. This is the primary command that Jesus calls us to obey. It is the great dignity to which you have been called when God created you "according to the image and likeness" of Christ, His only begotten Son. By striving to become what you are in God's love, you reach a state of inner harmony and oneness with God, your neighbor and the world around you. All God's creatures in whom He lives and moves, manifest your oneness with God and His creation in deep peace and joy.

Jesus Still Lives

Our faith in the resurrectional presence of Jesus Christ allows us to replace the towns of Galilee by our cities and countries of today. He is the same yesterday, today and always. He lives in you and me and in our material world. He walks along our sidewalks, in our woods, inside our prisons. He is still leaning over the maimed and the crippled, the epileptic and leprous, the depressed and hopeless of our world and is bringing His healing love. The incarnate Word of God becomes enfleshed among us again, each day. And He calls you to birth Him into being into your world as Mary brought Him forth at Bethlehem.

By His resurrectional life He lives within you, and through you will come alive in others. He wishes to extend His healing, loving presence into the rest of the broken world as you stretch out your loving hands united to His to bring His living presence to all you meet. Jesus has need of other human beings to become His Body, His hands and feet, His members. With them He can bring "all things to be reconciled through him and for him, everything in heaven and everything on earth" (Col 1:19).

The Call Of Christ

We can thrill at the thought of Jesus Christ needing us poor servants to bring Him alive into our world. Like the disciples, we too are overwhelmed that He has called us to follow Him. It took them a long time to understand the aim of Christ's incarnation and death. It took them a long time to understand that the Kingdom of Christ would not come into existence without not only the death of Christ and His resurrection but also their own death to selfishness and their rising to Christ's Spirit of love.

He asked of His disciples, and is asking of us each day in our morning aloneness with Him and in our touching Him throughout the day in recollection, that we turn away from self-centeredness by a *metanoia* or inner conversion. The values by which we live must be centered now completely on God as manifested through the workings of God's Word, Jesus Christ, whom we have consciously experienced as Lord and Savior in contemplative prayer.

Your Response

What will be your daily response to such a challenging invitation to follow Him in His glory? Will each day be a new birthing of Jesus and yourself into a new oneness, a new creation, He your Head, you His member? As you purify your heart of all selfishness and allow Him to enter into your life as your King and Lord, He will use your hands and feet, your eyes, your tongue, your whole being. He will work through you to bring others to know of the great love of the Father mirrored forth by His Son in His Spirit.

The birth, death and resurrection of Jesus cannot be separated in God's plan as it unfolded in history. Likewise as you experience the birth of Christ taking place within your heart each day in contemplative prayer, so you are to go forth and live your death and resurrection. You release the Christ-life within your life and the lives of those to whom you are privileged to go. You give in loving service, as Mary gave, out of the abundance of the Jesus she had experienced as she "treasured all these things and pondered them in her heart" (Lk 2:19–20).

IV

We Adore You, Oh Christ

There are three ways we can contemplate the world around us: we can see its power, its beauty and its grandeur. We can accordingly respond to our contemplation of the world by either exploiting it, enjoying it or accepting it in *awefull* contemplation. We, in the West, have learned in order to comprehend. With Bacon we too can say: "Knowledge is power." But the Hebrews bequeathed knowledge to us and to Christianity, in order to lead us to reverence, wonder and worship of God.

Adoration and worship are the climax of all true Christian prayer and contain all other elements such as petition, thanksgiving and sorrow. Yet in our pragmatic society we feel uncomfortable with those things which cannot be rendered immediately into something "profitable" to ourselves. Science has convinced us that with our human intellects we can solve all problems. We are the masters of the earth, and our own individual needs and interests are the ultimate criteria of what is right and wrong. We grow blind to intangible values of beauty, of things that stir us to silent wonder and awe without any immediate marketable value.

Evelyn Underhill, the English authority on mysticism, writes of the upward and outward look of humble and joyful admiration. She speaks of "awestruck delight in the splendour and beauty of God . . . in and for Himself alone, as the very colour of life; giving its quality of unearthly beauty to the harshest, most disconcerting forms and the dreariest stretches of experience. This is adoration: not a difficult religious exercise, but an attitude of the soul . . . What a contrast this almost inarticulate act of measureless adoration is to what Karl Barth calls the dreadful prattle of theology: 'Hallowed be Thy Name' . . . . Before that Name let the most soaring intellects cover their eyes with their wings and adore. Compared with this, even the coming of the Kingdom and the doing of the Will are side issues; articular demonstrations of the Majesty of the Infinite God, on whom all centers, and for whom all is done."

God Alone is God

God has given all of us talents and He expects us to use them. But our very use of them must contain that element of adoration whereby we place God in His awesome transcendence and ultimacy as the supreme Being, worthy of the complete sacrifice of ourselves to His glory. Prayer essentially is not going to God to receive things, gifts useful to our lives, or feelings that buoy us up and strengthen us to move out of meaninglessness. Prayer is ultimately our surrender of ourselves totally to God for His own sake and glory.

King David showed us how to pray in adoration and worship as he prayed to Yahweh in consecrating the treasures of his people to God's glory in the building of the Temple under Solomon:

May you be blessed, Yahweh . . . Yours, Yahweh, is the greatness, the power, the splendour, length of days, sovereignty. Yahweh; you are exalted over all, supreme. Riches and honour go before you, you are ruler of all, in your hand lie strength and power; in your hand it is to give greatness and strength to all. At this time, our God, we give you glory, we praise the splendour of your name. For who am I and what is my people to have the means to give so generously? All comes from you; from your own hand we have given them to you . . . Yahweh our God, this store we have provided to build a house for your holy name, all comes from your hand, all is yours.

Then David said to the whole assembly, 'Bless now Yahweh your God!' And the whole assembly blessed Yahweh, the God of their ancestors, and went on their knees to do homage to Yahweh (1Chr 29:10–20).

The greatest gift we can give to God is to be presence to Him in truth and in love, in worshipful surrender. Fr. Peter van Breeman in his book, *Called by Name*, underlines what our true talent is before God: "But the heart of our talents is not that we can preach, teach, do a work of art, important as these accomplishments are, they are only secondary. We do not know what talents Jesus had, but if he had any, he did not waste them. But the real talent Jesus had was to remain in God. If we lose the basic talent, all others are useless . . . The real talent is invisible to the eyes of men."

Wasting Time With God

Spending time as a loving presence to a husband, a wife, to one's children or to a friend cannot be valued in terms of doing but only in terms of "becoming" your true self in the love given and received. Contemplation, where nothing happens in concrete, measurable terms, may seem to be most impractical to the worldly minded. Understanding true adoration will purify our hearts and our minds from any errors that often creep into prayer.

We see this first aspect of adoration in the story of Moses encountering God in the burning bush. Moses saw a bush that was burning in the desert as he tended Jethro's flocks. His first impulse was one of curiosity. He wanted to comprehend something about God by his own rational powers. But God spoke to Moses and commanded him to strip himself of all his securities and meet Him in sheer faith. "Come no nearer. Take off your shoes, for the place on which you stand is holy ground" (Ex 3:5). And we read: "At this Moses covered his face, afraid to look at God."

This is the "mysterium tremendum" of Rudolph Otto. Job experienced this as he confronted the fullness of being in God as against his own sinfulness: "I knew you, then, only by hearsay; but now, having seen you with my own eyes, I retract all I have said, and in dust and ashes I repent" (Jb 42:5–6).

In true prayer we come into the presence of God who is over and beyond us, one whom we cannot possess by our own powers of intellect. We can know Him only by the "cloud of unknowing." In such experiential knowledge of God, He must take the initiative. But first we must remove all barriers that we have put up to prevent us from surrendering completely to God on His terms. Striving to possess the Unpossessable that makes all others possessions vain becomes a magnificent obsession for the pure of heart. Nietzsche once said: "A thing explained ceases to interest us; this is why God will always interest us."

Illumination and Transformation

We become true contemplatives in prayer, not when we advance toward God under our own power, but paradoxically, when we fall back in adoring humility before His transcendence. God is not a land to be conquered by our force, but a Holy Land which we approach with bare feet. We walk as Moses did, emptied of power.

When we are ready to relinquish our pre-conceived ideas about God, He will then reveal Himself to the meek and humble of heart. Moses before the burning bush could not seize the fire with his hands, nor can we bring God under our control. Yet God revealed Himself to Moses as fire, illuminating and transforming him into His prophet.

We too enter into God's illumination and transformation when we adore Him. We stand before Him in poverty of spirit. We say nothing, for what can we say before the Ineffable? What thought can we think that is worthy of Him who is the Incomprehensible? In adoration and worship we offer ourselves to this devouring Fire to be purified of all that is of our independent selves. God wishes to devour us. That is what a contemplative is: one who is devoured by God. Such a Christian is no longer separated from God but forms one being with Him. He merges as iron merges into fire to become fire. He becomes "light from Light." He becomes divinized by God's very own life, transfiguring him into a true child of God. He participates truly in the very nature of God (2 Pet 1:4).

Adoration demands a total surrender to God. It means destroying all images and idols that we have created of God and notions of how He should respond to us. C.S. Lewis well describes this in his *Letters to Malcolm*: "Only God Himself can let the bucket down into the depths in us. And on the other side, He must constantly work as the iconoclast. Every idea of Him we form, He must in mercy shatter. The most blessed result of prayer would be to rise thinking, 'But I never knew before. I never dreamed. . . .' I suppose it was at such a moment that Thomas of Aquinas said of all of his theology: 'It reminds me of straw.' "

True Adoration Saves Us from Error

True adoration based on humility can keep us from falling into aberrations in our prayer life. It recognizes both

God's allness and our inner beauty in God's creation of us. One such error is to use techniques in meditation, or even encounters with God, in order to gain peace of mind and greater efficiency in human creativity. True worship of God does lead us to peace of mind. The power of God within us should help us to become more creative. All too often, prayer techniques are taught devotees only as a means to enhance one's physical, psychological and spiritual being. Prayer then becomes a way to rid oneself of all sufferings, to become prosperous economically and to win friends and influence them. The cross is never mentioned nor is the shadow of sin within us.

Another erroneous view of prayer that true adoration can offset is that which comes from belonging to a very elite group of "saved" persons. Amos the prophet, eight centuries before Christ, railed against the Jewish people that thought merely being Jewish qualified them for being God's chosen ones. He prophesied through the mouth of Yahweh: "All the sinners of my people are going to perish by the sword, all those who say, 'No misfortune will ever touch us, nor even come anywhere near us' " (Am 9:10). The "once-saved-always-saved" type of Christian falls into this category and manifests a naive sense of true adoration and worship due to a basically self-centered security that fails to surrender to God's supremacy.

Some forms of Christianity stress too one-sidedly the corruption of mankind. True, adoration allows us to keep in happy tension the "already" and the "not yet." It preserves the absolutely gratuitous nature of God's saving grace along with our basic inherited sinfulness; yet it also declares that what God has created is not corrupt but remains always oriented toward a full participation in God's own nature. We can never lose the sublime destiny for which God has created us. True adoration always is built upon God's new covenant and His fidelity that loves us with an everlasting love.

Paul Tillich, the Protestant theologian, well captures the essence of adoration that keeps us freed from a trivial Christianity: "The marks of revelation—mystery, miracle, and ecstasy — are present in every true prayer . . . It is the presence of the mystery of being and an actualization of our ultimate concern. If it is brought down to the level of a conversation (or for that matter co-operation) between two beings, it is blasphemous and ridiculous." Chatty prayers that bring God's transcendence down to our level of values and vision of reality are remedied through true adoration and worship. This balances both God's transcendence and His gratuitous immanence. We humbly know in our sinfulness, that God madly loves us and lives within us as a triune community.

Yes, we are called to intimacy with God; but it is God who calls us and on His terms, not ours. Without humility there can be no true adoration. Where there is adoration, there is true humility and true prayer.

Adoration and God's Intimate Presence

Many times we feel adoration means a quaking and shuddering before a powerful God. Christianity brings the full synthesis to all religions and thus perfects them. It highlights both the otherness of God in His perfect ultimacy and independence of us and also His humility in desiring to share His eternal life with us. We share this life through our surrender to His holy will.

Moses typifies for us one who meets God in His awesome transcendence. Elijah leads us into an adoring, intimate communion with a tender, loving God. On Mount Sinai, in a theophany of terrifying thunder and lightning, God manifested to Moses His awesome holiness. Elijah heard God intimately present as a gentle, delicate voice from within.

Elijah stood before God ready to serve Him in his adoration and worship. He wanted to serve the Lord only. His response was to say, "As Yahweh lives, the God of Israel whom I serve . . ." (1 Kgs 17:1). In our adoration of God we too burn with zeal to serve. Yet God must first teach us that

He has no need of our puny services. The first and most important service we can render to God is attention and loving presence. God wishes us, as he showed Elijah, to stand before Him in inner attentiveness. God truly wishes to share His delights with His children (Pr 8:31). In adoration we are to be absorbed into the intimate, loving presence of the Lord. To worship and adore God is to lose one's time and one's whole being before God. It is a grace of wonder and childlike excitement. It is being joyous with Him and perceiving His loving, abiding presence.

To hear and accept God's word in obedience as a gentle whisper from within us, gives us our response: "Your word is joy to my heart" (Ps 119:111). Such a joy comes from true adoration that brings us to the discovery of God as the most tender Lover of all humanity. He is not outside us, but in Him we live and move and have our being (Ac 17:28).

When God creates us, He is not "another", standing outside of us as some other object, different from ourselves. Yet we are not God; we are different from Him. Adoration reconciles this seeming paradox of how God can be different from us and still not be "another", standing outside of us. Elijah learned this through the experience he had of the intimacy of God in all His gentle, delicate, loving presence to him on top of Mount Horeb. "And after the fire there came the sound of a gentle breeze. And when Elijah heard this, he covered his face with his cloak and went out and stood at the entrance of the cave" (1 Kgs 19:12–13).

In adoration we experience God's look of love in which He continually creates us according to His Word. He looks fondly with love upon us. As we adoringly surrender to His "still, silent voice", we become the being God wishes us to be. In that look of love we see our proper face, our real self. The look of a person is the open door into the depths of his/her heart. It is in the look of our loved ones that we discover ourselves and are loved by them. How much more true this is of God. He looks, and His gaze is one of perfect love, infinite tenderness, the closest intimacy. God looks at us, seeing all the possibilities that He is calling us to and invites us to accept His call.

True prayer is rooted in adoration and worship. It is the opening of the door of our hearts to let God enter and have complete dominance in our lives. It is to be penetrated completely by the look of God, which fills us with the desire to live always in the light of God's shining countenance. Union is born. There is the continued assurance, through contemplative prayer, of being loved infinitely and tenderly by God in each moment of life.

It has been said that to love serves for nothing, but it changes everything. The same is true of adoration. It has no cash-value; but it transforms everything into everlasting life. Adoration teaches us to hear God say continually: "I am your God and you are My child. Here is My eternity. My very own power and life, My sanctity, are yours. Let's put it all together with your daily, earthly life, with your poverty, even with your sinfulness and failures. Let us fulfill the potential I have placed within you to share My life."

V

Lord, Hear Us

Recently I was interviewed on a radio talk-program by a long distance telephone hook-up. After a brief explanation by myself, with the interviewer asking some broad questions about prayer, telephone lines were open to the listening audience who could ask direct questions about prayer. I was surprised how often the questions kept returning to the basic question of faith in God's willingness to answer our prayers and why, if He truly loves us, He does not always answer all that we ask Him for.

For many interested in contemplative prayer there can develop a faulty understanding of such a wordless, loving gaze upon God by deep faith, hope and love, without the medium of images and discursive dialogue with God. We might think that contemplative prayer is focused solely upon God. Therefore, according to such thinking, there should be no longer any room in a contemplative's prayer-life for a loving, concerning, petitional type of prayer for own's own needs or the needs of others.

We have been taught a doctrine that was formulated by Origen of the 3rd century in Alexandria. Prayer can focus upon four aims: there is the prayer of petition; prayer of thanksgiving; prayer of contrition or expiation; and prayer of adoration and worship. We could erroneously conceive such types of prayer as steps in a ladder leading to the highest form of communion with God, contemplation. Thus we might think that we are going backward to a "lower" level of prayer if we were to ask God for anything for ourselves or for others.

This is to mistake contemplation as being perfectly centered upon God and therefore automatically demanding no concern about others. It is true that petitional prayer is the most basic form of prayer we all learned from our mothers. It is found taught frequently in the New Testament, even by Jesus. He taught us to ask the Father anything in His name and it would be granted (Mt 21:22). He gave several parables; of the insistent neighbor asking for some bread in the middle of the night, of a widow plaguing a judge until he granted her petition etc. In the *Our Father* He taught us that we should turn to our Heavenly Father as He did during His earthly life and ask for our daily bread.

It is true that many times we could ask God for things, both for ourselves and for others, in a way that is self-centered. Our petition should be centered upon the glory of God by praying with the mind of Christ.

True petitional prayer is not prayer to ask God to change His mind when all our human efforts have failed. It is more an attitude of total dependence upon God for everything. We read in the letter of James: "It is all that is good, everything that is perfect, which is given us from above; it comes down from the Father of all light; with him there is no such thing as alteration, no shadow of a change. By his own choice he made us his children by the message of the truth so that we should be a sort of first-fruits of all that he had created" (Ja 1:16-18).

God's Creative Love

Many of our difficulties about prayer being answered by God or not stem from a faulty idea of God in His love for us. Emmanuel Kant, the German philosopher, expressed the skepticism so commonly found against petitional prayer. "It is said at once to be an absurd and presumptuous delusion to try by the insistent importunity of prayer, whether God might not be deflected from the plan of his wisdom to provide some momentary advantage for us."

Prayer is so often a cry of a human being in total weakness. "O God, come to my assistance!" God's plan of wisdom presupposes that He has given us freedom, not only to pray and to believe in His protective love, but to cooperate as we pray to do all we can do to bring about the fulfillment of the prayer. God is a Person, three Persons in a loving community of triune love. He wants to hear His children ask and thus reach a new awareness of knowledge of being in God's reality where He is truly God and we are His dependent children.

Are we to dismiss petitionary prayer as useless if God already is all-wise and all-knowing? Why does He need to hear it from us? Why not already begin to thank Him and short-cut bothering God? God surely does not need to hear our needs expressed; surely He is not deaf and therefore we need not shout with insistence! But such prayer presupposes that God is God and everything comes to us from Him. To be human is to recognize that one is not independent from God and others and cannot exist in total self-dependency. Prayer is not a call for help as much as the acknowledgement of the reality that we receive everything from God, our being, life and meaning, freedom and strength. We exist by God's grace.

We need petitionary prayer to express to ourselves and to others that we are, in the words of St. Irenaeus of the 2nd century, an empty receptacle to be filled by God's goodness.

God's creative love is forever unfolding within the context of our daily lives. It pleases God to give us the Kingdom.

He is now bringing about our happiness, our meaningfulness and enriching us with His participated goods. This is the dynamic vision Jesus had of His Father moving always into His daily life and creatively working out of love for Him. "My father goes on working, and so do I" (Jn 5:17).

God's uncreated energies of love invade your daily life at each moment. The world, from God's viewpoint, is a *one*. All creatures, through the creative inventiveness and cooperation of man working with God, were meant to be interrelated in a harmonious wholeness. Each part has its proper place within the whole universe. Each creature depends on and gives support to all the others in one great body, all of which has been created in and through God's Word.

This wonderful, creating God is not only the powerful, transcendent Creator who stands above and outside of all His creation, but He is the immanent force that lives inside of every creature. "In him we live and move and have our being" (Ac 17:28). He fills the heavens and the underworld. It is impossible to escape from His creative, sustaining Spirit (Ps.139:7).

A World Groaning in Bondage

However, it is not easy for us to offer petitions according to the mind of God so that our will is always one with the will of God. It is revelation through Holy Scripture that teaches us what happened to God's creation which He saw was very good. The harmony in all things gave way to chaos and dissension, filling human beings with a bias toward self-love. We find resistance in our prayers to pray for God's will to be done as we strive to receive from God only what we think is for our own good or the good of others.

But God condemned sin in the flesh through the death and resurrection of Jesus Christ. Now you can be assured that you have an almighty High-Priest who intercedes before the Father's throne on your behalf. You can now offer petitions in His name and believe, as Jesus teaches us, that the Father will answer such prayers. For we no longer pray out of a "carnal mind" but a Spirit-filled mind.

You offer your God-given talents to work in a oneness, a *synergy* of two wills become one. You surrender to God's immanent and active presence in all creatures as you strive to put yourself "inside" of God's holy will. You place yourself at the complete disposal of God who weaves new patterns of existence into the most perfect possible work of art. What is impossible with man becomes possible with God. We go to prayer to touch the trembling hands of God striving to become one will with His will of supreme creativity. It does not mean that you are adding *your* power to God's power. It is to enter into a universe bursting with an infinity of possibilities as we seek to surrender to live for God's glory.

You are stretching out of the darkness of egotistic death to embrace God's ever fresh, vibrant life. You are always to live in the spring of His loving activity; never in the winter of our frigid selfishness.

Discerning Principles

Let us look at some principles concerning how to pray as we ought. 1. First, there is required in all prayer a discernment of our desires and needs. Is it the good Spirit of God's love directing us in any given form of prayer, or a spirit of worldliness and self-centeredness? 2. Immaturity in the spiritual life is seen primarily as a self-absorption of what we need, especially focusing almost exclusively on our physical and psychological needs. There are the needs that are very evident and satisfying to ourselves so that we do not have to endure much suffering. 3. After we have discerned what to ask for, we can measure the true sign of our maturity in the spiritual life by examining how we offer our petitions to God

I used to think that in true contemplative prayer I had no need to petition God for anything. This, I reasoned, was to go backward to a "lower" level of prayer. If we were to ask God for "things" in a stage of prayer where our faith, hope and love have developed through years of mental prayer, would this be not believing that God already knows all my needs? All I had to do, therefore, was to begin to thank Him for arranging all things so "sweetly." I see now that petitional prayer is a vital part of a contemplative's life. By allowing God to touch us more deeply, we are able to stand aside and watch our false ego operate in contrast to God's allness in our lives. Our discernment of whether we pray or not to God for fulfillment of a need is not followed by a petitional attitude that we want God to do what we discern He must do. What follows discernment of asking God to fulfill our petitions is a surrendering of our every desire to embrace God's will in lively faith, abandoning trust and childlike love.

4. In such a stance we can see how it is proper and right to ask God for things for ourselves and for others. We can see that petitional prayer also embraces thanksgiving, confession of our unworthiness before God and, above all, adoration and worship, the essence of contemplative prayer.

This step in petitional prayer requires an integration of our whole self under God's supreme dominion. Your inner eye, as Jesus said, becomes a single eye. You are "single-minded." Your magnificent obsession, as that of Jesus in His prayer to the Father, is not your will but His be done unto His glory.

5. Grounded in such a holistic perspective of prayer, you can then move to the element found so often in the Gospel as taught by Jesus. You storm Heaven with *persistence*. You *soak* yourself or the one you are praying for with prayer, "fiery" prayer, as St. John Cassian of the 4th century called it. You accompany your continued prayer with a further discernment and testing of what you initially judged as a need. You clarify that need.

6. To avoid seeking your own selfish desires or convenience in petitional prayer, keep a check on your inner and

external concentration upon God and His glory to avoid dispersion. Fasting can often give our petitions a "bite," a real dying to selfishness. Fasting can move into any moderate control over thoughts, desires and sense appetites that are being directed by your false ego, rather than by God's Spirit.

7. As you continue to pray for certain needs, be ready to act on what you already discern God is asking you to do. For example, to see a certain doctor; to stop smoking; to exercise more, etc.

8. The most important element that links petitional prayer to true contemplation is your continued praying in a child-like abandonment to embrace God's holy will. God truly always answers your prayers when you pray in the *name* and the *presence* of Jesus and His Spirit, as you put on His mind of oneness with the Father.

Pray, but also surrender your petition to God in a deep faith that the good you are praying for is being granted as Jesus tells us. "Everything you ask and pray for, believe that you have it already, and it will be yours" (Mk 11:24; also Mt.9:23). Your faith in God's goodness and infinite love for you becomes greater than your desired need. You *believe* God is answering your prayer.

Glenn Clark writes: "The faith that shuts the mouths of lions is more than a pious hope that they will not bite." You pray with child-like confidence that God, our Father, will grant what is best for you. No longer are you *asking* for this or that. You now stand in confidence to receive from God's loving hands what He knows will be best for you.

As you focus totally on God and His deep and penetrating fatherly love for you, picture yourself receiving His gifts of love. You *see* from God's loving perspective. You become full of peace, joy, love as your praise rises to God, even in silent worship of total surrender to God's control over your life and all your needs. You are seeking first the Kingdom of God and literally all other things will be given to you (Lk 12:31).

You can see that true petitional prayer is not inferior to contemplative prayer. It need not be selfish nor the prayer of only a beginner in the spiritual life. In it all forms of prayer coalesce and lead to true contemplation which is wordless surrender and worship—the essence of authentic love and the sign of our being divinized into children of God through the Spirit of the risen Jesus.

Intercessory Prayer

It remains to discuss the peak of petitional prayer, i.e., intercessory prayer. As you contemplate God's amazing love in your life and in His designs for others, you are moved by the Spirit to be concerned for the needs of all persons who somehow or other enter your life. Loving concern and merciful compassion toward the needy are signs that you live "in truth and love." It is a faulty understanding of prayer that ignores interceding for the needs of others. This is where Church is formed, especially around the Eucharistic table, and meets in loving outreach toward any member of the human race in need. It is to unite your heart with the heart of the risen Jesus Christ, who alone, as our High-Priest, can intercede for all before the throne of the Father.

You have been born in Baptism to be a sharer in the high-priesthood of Christ (1 P 2:4,9). Being a part in Christ, possessing a "place" within the Body of Christ, you share in the responsibility of being a mediator or co-presence of God to others. God has need of you to make Himself present to others. You intercede for them in their needs because you are privileged to know them and be concerned about them.

Guiding Principles

Here are some guiding principles for your intercessory prayer. 1. *Guided by love*, you intercede on behalf of another or others out of compassionate love. 2. You are ready also to do more than merely voice a prayer to God. Abbé Huvelin wrote: "You will never do much for people, except by suffering for them." Real intercessory prayer is an act of love, ready to sacrifice oneself for the good of another. 3. *Grounded in faith,* you need to believe in the unconditional love of God who wishes to give His children all they need for their well being. 4. Pray for the whole person and all that is best for his/her spiritual development and happiness. 5. Be persistent in your pleading before God.

Exercise in Intercessory Prayer

Take this exercise in intercessory prayer. Place before your mind three persons for whom you wish to pray. One is your loved one; the second is an indifferent person, perhaps some world leader or person of influence; and, lastly, a person who considers you an enemy or at least shows animosity toward you.

Cover each person with God's love for him/her. See that person gathered lovingly into the Father's arms. Know that for that person Jesus has truly died. This person is your brother/sister and meant to be one with you in the Body of Christ. Send positive suggestions of God's love and yours also to that person. See and experience intercessory prayer as a continued widening circle of burning love where you put on the mind of Christ and seek to be all things to all persons to win them to Christ.

St. Paul exhorts us to such intercession: "My advice is that, first of all, there should be prayers offered for everyone—petitions, intercession and thanksgiving—and especially for kings and others in authority, so that we may be able to live religious and reverent lives in peace and quiet. To do this is right, and will please God our savior: he wants everyone to be saved and reach full knowledge of the truth" (1 Tim 2:1-5).

VI

The Oasis of Tears

The final goal of all Christian prayer centers upon adoration and worship of God as our Supreme Being, the Center
of our life. He alone is God and deserving of all our love. But
a very overlooked aspect of authentic Christian prayer, at
least in our modern world, is that of confessing our brokenness and sinfulness before the Lord in a humble stretching
out by His power. This confession of brokenness impels us to
leave the world of our illusory, self-created desires and move
into God's real world of love, peace and joy in harmony with
God and His entire, created world.

We fear too much a seeming negativity in our prayer-life.
It is true; God is very positive and life-giving. But there is a
force within us that should not be there. It is really existent,
proved by the fact that we so often are influenced by its
power from within us. In order to be healed, we must be
persuaded that we are sick and not what we should be. We
must receive God's grace that summons us to awaken from

our sleep, from our life spent so much living in darkness. To receive such a grace takes discipline and honesty. In a word, it requires an inner transformation away from our false self to move into humility and the discovery by God's illumination of our beautiful true self in Christ. Much needs to be demythologized from early Christians, especially those of the East. They stressed so much the absolute necessity on our part to be in touch with our darkness and nothingness through a dread of yielding to the enemy that lived inside ourselves. This they called *Penthos*. It was meant to be a constant element in all prayer, whether individual or public, liturgical or private. For they knew that sin in us prevents us from experiencing God's great love for us. That love was experienced only when we had the honesty to confess our inauthenticity and our many turnings away from the goodness and love of God for us.

One of the great graces that I have received through my contact with Eastern Christian writers, especially those of the early Church, is the utter conviction of the necessity of recognizing our sinful condition. In a state of constant conversion or turning of oneself totally to God as the source of all strength, we must cry out continually for His healing and transformation of such brokenness. This accent is summarized succinctly by Abbot Pimen: "Weep; there is no other way to perfection."

In the West we all too readily think of one of the principal elements of prayer, that of sorrow and contrition for sins, as an attitude we seek to put on in preparing for the rite of reconciliation or in a retreat. Paul Tillich captures something of the keen Eastern Christian insight in regard to mourning over the human brokenness that is in all of us in his essay, "The Eternal Now." He writes: "It is the act of the whole person in which he separates himself from elements of his being, discarding them into the past as something that no longer has any power over the present."

When we begin to live more consciously and more interiorly, we make contact with what St. Paul describes as "sin which lives inside my body" (Rm 7:23). Sin becomes something more than our deliberate acts of transgression against a divine law. We can learn much from early Christianity and those saints of the desert who had passed beyond the extrinsic aspects of the law. They had entered into a deep self-knowledge of the inner movements of the "heart" as well as a deep consciousness of God's very immediate and tender love for them. In a word, sin for them was anything that was an obstacle to joyfully living the good news of the Paschal Mystery.

Claiming One's Brokenness

True Christian prayer possesses four main characteristics: adoration or worship of God; petition; thanksgiving and sorrow unto forgiveness. Let us explore this latter quality of prayer. Adoration is our attitude when we encounter God as supreme through faith, hope and love. You understand by God's infusion and in your experience of the *allness* of God that you are sheer gift from God's goodness. Rudolph Otto in his classic, *The Idea of the Holy*, shows how adoration of God in His awesome transcendence fills us with the *mysterium tremendum*, the awe of the Prophet Isaiah, which he experienced as he was lifted up to the throne of God to encounter the holiness of God (Is 6:1–3).

But the confession of our unworthiness and sinfulness that Isaiah also experienced flows out of adoration. "What a wretched state I am in! I am lost, for I am a man of unclean lips . . . and my eyes have looked at the King, Yahweh Sabaoth" (Is 6:5). For one who lives superficially such a confession of one's unworthiness before God has little meaning. But for those who with St. Paul enter deeply into their consciousness and even unconsciousness, a whole inner world of fragmentation and darkness opens up.

Have you in prayer experienced such an inner duality as St. Paul experienced when he wrote:

> . . . but I am unspiritual; I have been sold as a slave
> to sin. I cannot understand my own behaviour. I

fail to carry out the things I want to do, and I find myself doing the very things I hate . . . and so the thing behaving in that way is not my self but sin living in me . . . When I act against my will, then, it is not my true self doing it, but sin which lives in me . . . What a wretched man I am! Who will rescue me from this body doomed to death? Thanks be to God through Jesus Christ our Lord! (Rm 7:14–25).

A Self-Created Prison

When we do take time to move into deeper prayer, we discover within ourselves two centers that vie with each other to control our value systems. There is the false ego or the Kingdom of Mammon that is characterized as afraid, hostile to the outside world, proud, greedy, deceitful, guilt-laden, a feeling of inferiority mixed with an aggressive attacking pride. The other center is the true self that has been made by God according to His own image and likeness. This true self is noble, self-sacrificing, loving toward God and neighbor and radiates humility, peace and joy in all its loving relationships to God's real world.

The false ego is illusory and has been created by ourselves through guilt and the fear of not being loved by God and others. We create such an inner prison every time we move away from true love and enter into a state of self-centeredness. We build the prison; we are the prisoner; but we are also the jailer who holds the key to open the prison door if we should wish. Evelyn Underhill describes this self-created prison: "By false desires and false thoughts man has built up for himself a false universe: as a mollusk, by the deliberate and persistent absorption of lime and rejection of all else, can build up for itself a hard shell which shuts it from the external world, and only represents in a distorted and unrecognizable form the ocean from which it was obtained. This hard and wholly unnutritious shell, this one-sided secretion of the surface consciousness, makes as it were a little cave of illusion for each separate soul."

It is God's love above all that shows us how tightly constrained we are within the prison of our selfishness and egoism. If we have the courage to turn within and, in silence and honesty, look into the tomb of our inner darkness, the light of God's tender love illumines us. Ever so softly and healingly, interior tears well up in our spiritual eyes. We whisper in the depths of our heart: "Have mercy on me, O God, in Your goodness" (Ps 51:1).

Authentic Conversion

In such inner quieting we gently yield to the operations of the Holy Spirit who shows us what needs continual healing from deep within us. We see our fragmentation and we sorrow at seeing what could have been. We experience how great and tender and lasting has been God's love for us and we see our ingratitude. We feel caught in a prison of darkness and yet we can see a delicate ray of light leading us through the crack of *metanoia,* a conversion to the Lord Jesus.

The words of the Prophet Joel become the atmosphere in which we live with urgency as we begin to experience our own inadequacies to set ourselves free from all falsity within us by our own power:

. . . come back to me with all your heart,
fasting, weeping, mourning.
Let your hearts be broken, not your garments torn,
turn to Yahweh your God again,
for he is all tenderness and compassion,
slow to anger, rich in graciousness,
and ready to relent (Jl 2:12–13).

As we sit within our inner desert like the desert Fathers of earlier centuries, we learn to yield to the indwelling presence of Jesus Christ. The Divine Physician alone can bring life and give us that life more abundantly. We cry out as often as we can, day and night, with distrust in our powers to save ourselves, but with childlike trust in Jesus the Healer: "Lord, Jesus Christ, Son of God, have mercy on me, a sinner." This demands a life of reflection, of sensitive inner knowledge in the light of God's indwelling presence and infinite love. In His light we see our darkness.

In that darkness we honestly recognize our guilt and sinfulness. We claim it as our own without justification or rationalization. We are broken and we need God's mercy. We are sinners and have gone astray. The spirit of compunction or abiding sorrow for our godless past and the fear of a future without God strangely enough allows us to humbly contact God. God gives Himself to the weak, the poor, the needy. He looks upon the lowliness of His children who have entered into an experiential knowledge of their creaturehood.

This is the spirit found in all Christian liturgies as the faithful, through their own individual fragmentation, bring a broken world before the merciful God. It is to ask for inner healing of all that is false and proud and not loving. This is a vital part of all our individual prayer before God. It is this that determines the depth of our true and effective conversion to the Lord.

There cannot be any true conversion, which is a turning toward God as the only center of our value system, unless there is a breaking of our pride and self-centeredness. This is the first step of a conversion. It shows us that the Christian life is a constant conversion or a turning away from the false world of our own creation. Thus we can see why one of the elements in all authentic Christian prayer is a recognition of the inauthenticity which is guiding our lives. This is the sorrow and repentance that should be a part of all true prayer.

An Existential Dread

Thomas Merton develops the concept of an existential dread from the writings of Gabriel Marcel, the French Catholic philosopher. He writes: "When we are at rest, we find ourselves almost inevitably put in the presence of our own inner emptiness, and this very emptiness is in reality intolerable to us. But there is more. There is the fact that through this emptiness we inevitably become aware of the misery of our condition, a 'condition so miserable,' says Pascal, 'that nothing can console us when we think about it carefully.' Hence the necessity of diversion."

Merton places the importance of dread upon the realization of our own infidelity to a personal demand, the failure to meet a challenge or to fulfill a certain possibility which demands to be met and fulfilled. "It (the sense of dread) is the sense of defection and defeat that afflicts a man who is not facing his own inner truth and is not giving back to life, to God and to his fellow man, a fair return for all that has been given him." Such dread is most important for our spiritual growth, provided we confront it and become filled with a "holy disgust" for having spent so much time eating the husks of swine.

Such dread and existential anxiety cannot be removed by resorting to some juridicial effect obtained in the reception of the sacraments, without involving our own complete upheaval and regeneration by God's grace to become what God has always desired us to be. In the deepest reaches of such inner agony that St. John of the Cross describes so well in his work, *Dark Night of the Soul*, such dread becomes a wrestling with our nothingness and doubt that assails our integrity and religious identity. We seem to be lost on a dark ocean and have no direction or light to guide us.

The proud person will not persevere in such inner strife of faith. Instead, he will seek to escape the darkness and feeling of nothingness, and seek in prayer and busy activities the distractions that will perpetuate the myth that he is in charge. Dread divests us of any sense of self-importance. It is a therapeutic cleansing of ourselves by God's Spirit of all remnants of a false world. This is a necessary step before one can live in God's real world of love and self-sacrifice.

Second Movement in a Conversion

The second aspect of humility in any true Christian conversion is the positive enlightenment that results when we yield to God's grace in our brokenness and begin to live our new life-in-Christ. Its initial stage is a stretching out to possess the new life promised us by Christ (Jn 10:10). The darkness within your heart begins to turn into light as you stretch out to make contact with your Lord and Savior. Christ lives deep down, within your "heart." He promised you and me that He and the Father would come and abide within us (Jn 14:23). At the center of your being you can still fall down and confess your belief that Jesus Christ is the son of God. You can cry out to Him that you are broken in body, soul and spirit and need His healing love.

He releases His Holy Spirit who reveals that Jesus Christ, the Image of the Father, loves you unto the madness of the cross. "For me He dies!" (Ga 2:20) becomes for you an experience that leads you into the awesome presence of the Heavenly Father as perfect holiness, beauty and love. You experience the pulling together of your frightened spirit, your scattered mind. Guilt and fears, anxieties, hatred, feelings of inferiority and judgment against others dissolve in the tears of your own joyful reconciliaton to God's immense love. You discover yourself as if for the first time. You enter into a "birthing" of your beautiful, true self in Christ. You feel as though nothing on the face of the earth, not even death, can ever take you from the love of God (Rm 8:34).

You can see how important is this confrontation with the inner darkness and nothingness of your false self. Such a confrontation urges you on to leave that world of illusory desires that you built up, in order to enter into God's real world. You learn now to yield to God's healing love in prayer. You cease to "do" anything in prayer for now your prayer is your total, true self, joyfully surrendering to God's holy will. As you surrender to His love, and His peace pours over you like a soft rain falling gently on dry ground, the powers God placed within you as seeds unto divinization crack open. Your potential for *being* expands into a realized consciousness. You feel in the depths of your being a new transformation taking place.

Powers to love, to-be-towards God, towards yourself in a healthy way and towards others, open up slowly like the locked-in petals of a bedewed rose. Gently they let go to expose a new harmony of many things captured in the union of one flower of exquisite beauty. The chaotic past, those dried bones of yester-year, receive the soft breath of God's Spirit of love and they become enfleshed into your newly transformed being.

You come out of the past. ". . . feet and hands bound with bands of stuff and a cloth round his face. Jesus said, 'Unbind him, let him go free' " (Jn 11:44). As you sit in prayer crying out to Jesus Lord to show His merciful love, you receive an expanded consciousness that floods your entire being. You feel the body, soul, spirit relationships within you come together in an integrated, whole person. You experience the divine, uncreated energies of God's triadic life flowing through you in every part, on every level. You are alive with God's life.

You never want to return to the dark world of illusions and of selfishness. Now you want to live in God's real world that allows you to live in loving harmony with God, neighbor and with all God's creatures. You have been made by God to share in His Being. He is Love, and when you love Him and you are loved by Him in return, you *are* what you were made for. Through the healing power of Christ's Spirit of Love experienced in prayer, and in the sacramental encounter with Christ as Healer in the Rite of Reconciliation and in the Holy Eucharist, you know a new-founded peace and joy pervading your entire life (Ga 5:22; Ph 4:4).

Practicing Compunction

If such sorrow and stretching out from your brokenness and false reality are essential elements in your prayer-life, how can you put this into practice? We have already seen the double movement in a conversion. One is a dread and disgust with the darkness in which we have been living. We recognize our ingratitude toward God who has loved us with such perfect and holy love. The other is to enter into the light of God's new life. We accept this new life to the degree that we sincerely resolve to leave behind the darkness, and surrender completely to live in God's will, which is to live in love toward God and neighbor.

Each day will unearth from the depths of our being certain areas of darkness. These dark areas still rise up with their ugly hydra heads out of the past, from out of our repressed hurts and fears of the ghosts of yester-years. We need no longer be slaves of the past, of our sins and failures, of the hurts and seething angers because of what others have done to us. There is only this present moment as the Holy Spirit rips off the false posturing and phony masks that have created an illusion out of the past.

What a healing of life's hurts can come from experiencing this personalized love of the triune God who dwells within us! Such healing can come daily as we sit, deeply in prayer and allow God's love to heal past brokenness. It can come through healing in a praying group as we join our faith to that of loving Christians. Such Christian prayer brings the powerful intercession of Jesus to intercede with the Father to remove any darkness and bring us into the light of a oneness with Him and the Body of Christ. Healing of such darkness can come through reception of the sacraments, especially the Rite of Reconciliation and the Eucharist.

Each evening we can also set up a prayer-session that would highlight the encountering of our darkness to have it dissolved by the light of God's loving presence. Such an exercise could consist of four points. After placing yourself in the living presence of God by an act of faith, adoration, hope and love, first begin by praising God. Thank Him in detail for all His loving gifts and acts toward you that day and throughout your entire life. Secondly, ask that the Father and the Lord Jesus release their Spirit to enlighten you to get in touch with your brokenness of that day.

Thirdly, go through the day and seek honestly to be in touch with your feelings of that day. Give honest expression to those feelings. Just how did you feel then toward those who may have hurt you? How do you feel now? Let any anger come forth. Don't be afraid to complain before God. But also don't be afraid to feel some disgust toward your false self. You are seeking an absolutely untrammeled self-revelation in God's loving presence. He is beyond anything that might hurt or offend Him. He loves you with an everlasting love and will never forsake you. Stand spiritually naked before Him. "Have mercy on me, O God, in your goodness, in your great tenderness wipe away my faults; wash me clean of my guilt, purify me from my sin" (Ps 51:1–2).

Fourthly, stretch out to the Lord Jesus, your Divine Physician, and cry in urgency that He come and touch you. Let the light of the risen Savior pour upon you. See Him come in all His glorious healing love to lead you out of your darkened prison. "Lazarus, come forth!" Imagine Jesus touching you in those relationships or feelings that keep you bound into a prison of self-pity and of pride. See yourself rising from your created world of unreality to enter joyfully into God's real world of love and peace and joy.

Is there in this life any other way to experience the true love of God except in contrast to our brokenness? How can God heal us by His love if we have not been broken in our ignorance of not having been loved by Him and others? How can we understand what God's presence means unless we have experienced His absence? How can we experience the Prodigal Father unless we first have experienced what a prodigal son or daughter means? Truly, "happy are those who mourn: they shall be comforted."

VII

The Inner Chamber

I always feel privileged and happy to preach or write about our Lord Jesus. It seems that, for all of us who hear a sermon about Him, there are as many representations of Jesus as there are listeners or readers. Would the real Jesus come forth? I guess we would have to be Jesus or the Heavenly Father or the Holy Spirit in order fully to comprehend the fullness of Jesus Christ and who He is for us.

St. Paul prayed often, as we should: "All I want is to know Christ and the power of his resurrection and to share his sufferings by reproducing the pattern of his death" (Ph 3:10). Jesus Himself promised to give us eternal life and even described it in terms of our possibility of knowing Him and the Father. "And eternal life is this: to know, the only true God and Jesus Christ whom you have sent" (Jn 17:3).

Creating an Idol

Perhaps one reason we do not fall more deeply in love with Him and surrender more completely in loving obedience to Him as our indwelling Word, is that we pray to an idol we have created. To pray to a Jesus created out of our own "carnal mind" is to pray to a non-reality or at most to a figment of our imagination. Our false ego may exploit in prayer the real Jesus, who died for us and calls us to total submission to His Lordship, in order that we may receive from Him that which will only separate us farther from Him. Thank God such prayers go unanswered, a loving gesture of our Heavenly Father who truly loves us in Christ (Jn 16:27) to give us only what is unto our perfect happiness.

True Devotion to the Sacred Heart

Nowhere in Western Christian piety do we find a clearer example of intimate devotion to Christ (not always bringing us into greater union and obedience to Him) than in the Western devotion to the Sacred Heart. Western Christianity understands from Holy Scripture the meaning of the human heart as a symbol, depicting in Christ both God's love for us in His divinity and in His humanity. Western mystics, especially within the Cistercian and Dominican traditions, were fond of entering into the pierced heart of Christ on the cross and there they experienced the "furnace" of divine love for humanity.

St. Margaret Mary Alacoque, a Visitandine contemplative at Parey-le-Monial in France in the 17th century, did much through her visions to shape Western devotion to the Sacred Heart of Jesus. She described her interior vision of the Sacred Heart that has constituted the visible symbols of what we associate with devotion to the Sacred Heart:

> "The divine Heart was represented to me as upon a throne of fire and flames. It shed rays on every

side, brighter than the sun and transparent as crystal. The wound which He received on the cross appeared there visibly. A crown of thorns encircled the divine Heart and it was surmounted by a cross."

We are all familiar with the popular aspects of devotion to the Sacred Heart of Jesus. Perhaps these concrete images can become, as we grow in deeper prayer, a real obstacle to true devotion to Christ. In our youth there were the pictures and statues of Jesus showing us His heart surrounded with fire and a crown of thorns with a sword penetrating the heart. We faithfully made the nine First Fridays. Novenas to the Sacred Heart preceded our formal consecration of ourselves and the world to the Sacred Heart on the feast in June. The official prayers of the church referred to the Sacred Heart as "It", but *it* was always capitalized!

A Biblical Christ

We do not want to lessen the main object of devotion to the Sacred Heart as the veneration of God's infinite love for us manifested in the suffering Jesus and our own return of love in consecration and reparation. Perhaps if we turn, as our Eastern Christian brethren have done down through the centuries, to Scripture, we will have the basis for a more "total" devotion to Jesus, the Lover of all of us. We will perhaps lose something of the undesirable, limiting and grossly materialistic aspects of the devotion as presented in the picture of a physical heart, all burning. Instead we will be called into the mystery of the God-Man, as totally God and totally Man, loving us to the madness of the cross.

We will forsake the over-emphasis on the cheap, saccharine aspects of an effeminate Jesus and discover the objective Jesus of the Gospel account who appears not so much as a "Prisoner of love" but as the Suffering Servant of Yahweh. We will recapture in our prayer the beautiful title of the Eastern Fathers given to Jesus as the *Philanthropos*, the Lover of mankind.

A New Heart

God had promised His people of the Old Testament that He would cleanse them with clean water and give them a new heart and a new spirit.

> I shall pour clean water over you and you will be cleansed; I shall cleanse you of all your defilement and all your idols. I shall give you a new heart, and put a new spirit in you; I shall remove the heart of stone from your bodies and give you a heart of flesh instead (Ez 36:25–26).

The heart in scriptural language is the seat of human life, of all that touches us in the depths of our personality: all affections, passions, desires, knowledge and thoughts. It is in our "heart" that we meet God in an I-Thou relationship. The heart, therefore, in scriptural language and as used by the Fathers of the desert of the Christian East, is the center of our being, that which directs us in our ultimate values and choices. It is the inner chamber where in secret the heavenly Father sees us through and through. It is where we attain inner honesty, integration and "purity of heart." In a word, it is the spaceless "place" where we encounter the Risen Lord Jesus as love poured out for us individually. It was in his heart that St. Paul daily encountered his loving Savior so that he could write: "I have been crucified with Christ, and I live now not with my own life but with the life of Christ who lives in me. The life I now live in this body I live in faith: faith in the Son of God who loved me and who sacrificed himself for my sake" (Ga 2:19–20).

A Symbol of Focus

How can we understand such a symbol as that of the *heart* to mean our deepest levels of consciousness and inner awareness, as the place where we meet God and where God's greatest love for us is met in the flaming love of His Son, Jesus Christ? Because of our "being-in-the-world," we are basically creatures who are not naturally, at all times, focused upon God in consciousness that He is our beginning and our end. We are being pulled in all directions by persons, things and events that clamor for our attention. We need to have a "focus" in order that our deepest relationship with God in an intimate, personal, loving union may not be too diffuse and abstract. We need a concrete presence in which our loving relationship with God may command the center of our consciousness and awareness and thus exert maximum influence on our thoughts, words and actions.

Our human heart is both a physical organ and a basic symbol of our existence in life. Even more, the heart symbolizes our transcendence beyond the world, the inner stretching power within our spirit to go toward God in thought and love. We are commanded to love God with our whole heart, our whole mind, our whole strength (Dt 6:6). Yahweh speaks through the prophet Jeremiah: "When you seek me you shall find me, when you seek me with all your heart" (Jer 29:13).

God became incarnate for love of us in Christ Jesus. Jesus as Man possesses a human heart. That heart can become for us the beautiful symbol, not only of His human love for us unto a human death, but also of His divine love. It is the image of the Heavenly Father's love for us manifested through the Holy Spirit in the human heart of Christ. We are very scriptural when we use the heart as the place where we encounter God in all His burning love for each of us. It is the place where we meet Him with all our strengths, God's gifts to us, but also with all our brokenness and sinfulness that cry out for healing from God. It is in the heart of Christ that the "new creation" or "the new man," is effected.

A Pure Heart

But when we come to prayer we realize that we are not quite yet one with Christ, a new creation. God meant the first man and first woman to walk in His loving presence, communicating with God in the coolness of evening. "He put his own light in their hearts to show them the magnificence of his works . . . Their eyes saw his glorious majesty and their ears heard the glory of his voice" (Si 17:8, 11).

But man lost the presence of God in his heart. Instead of light, darkness covered his heart, his consciousness of his identity in relationship to God. He had been created with a hunger for God's beauty, made according to God's image and likeness (Gn 1:26). God's face would be uncovered as men and women looked into the face of Jesus. "To have seen me is to have seen the Father," Jesus said (Jn 14:9). But to know the "heart" of Jesus, the deepest reaches of His consciousness in His loving and self-giving to us, He would pour out His Spirit into our hearts with His love (Rm 5:5).

Knowledge as experience in love of the "breadth and the length, the height and the depth" of the love of Christ which is beyond all knowledge (Ep 3:18), would come through the outpouring of His Spirit, as Jesus promised.

> If any man is thirsty, let him come to me! Let the man come and drink who believes in me! As scripture says: From his breast shall flow fountains of living water. He was speaking of the Spirit which those who believed in Him were to receive; for there was no Spirit as yet, because Jesus had not yet been glorified (Jn 7:37–39).

That Spirit, when released in our hearts after Jesus was raised from the dead, would fulfill what Jesus promised: ". . . the Advocate, the Holy Spirit, whom the Father will send in my name, will teach you everything and remind you of all I have said to you" (Jn 14:26). Above all, when we do not know how to pray in a deeper, surrendering way, the Spirit of Jesus comes to help us in our weakness. ". . . the Spirit himself expresses our plea in a way that could never be put into words . . ." (Rm 8:27).

The Love of Jesus

Jesus becomes God's Light shining before us most brilliantly when He is dying on the cross out of His infinite love for each of us. When the hill of Calvary was covered with darkness as of night and the Light of God's presence seemed totally extinguished, then the Light burst forth with the awesome glory of God covering that mangled body of Jesus. He was stripped of all beauty and comeliness. He screamed out in His terrifying abandonment by His Father.

Still there is more light to shine. Jesus has still more to show us, more of Himself to pour out for love of us in total emptying.

> When they came to Jesus, they found he was already dead, and so instead of breaking his legs one of the soldiers pierced his side with a lance; and immediately there came out blood and water. This is the evidence of one who saw it—trustworthy evidence and he knows he speaks the truth—and he gives it so that you may believe as well (Jn 19:33–35).

That emptied heart of Jesus, the Lover of mankind is the symbol of the total, self-giving Jesus. He images to us in human form, suffering unto death, the depth of love that the Heavenly Father has for each one of us through His Spirit of love. Before He freely went to His death, He "opened" up His "heart," His consciousness in the depths of His self-giving to us in the Last Supper.

A Eucharistic Love

When Jesus gathers His disciples together for a last meal, He is described in the New Testament as experiencing great excitement in His heart. He has now reached a peak moment in His life. Everything from the cave of Bethlehem, the small home in Nazareth, the desert temptations, the previous few years of exhausting travels to preach to and heal the multitudes has led to this moment.

> . . . . and Jesus knew that the hour had come for
> him to pass from this world to the Father. He had
> always loved those who were his in the world, but
> now he showed how perfect his love was (Jn 13:1).

Periodically during His public life this flaming love in His heart to accomplish what His Father had sent Him to do would flare out in words of ardent longing. "I have come to bring fire to the earth and how I wish it were blazing already! There is a baptism I must still receive, and how great is my distress till it is over! " (Lk 12:49–50). His baptism would be of water and blood poured out from His loving heart, the heart of a suffering God imaged in Jesus. When the spear would open His heart and there would pour forth the last drops of water and blood, then Jesus' work would be consummated. "It is accomplished" (Jn 19:30). What is? The end of the Incarnation, the reason why God had pitched His tent among us (Jn 1:14). God in man has now finally spoken His definitive Word in Jesus Christ. St. John standing at the foot of the cross has nothing to say. He invites us to "see" the Word being spoken clearly, telling us at that moment of God's infinite love for us. The horrendous folly of the sufferings of Christ is sheer nonsense except in terms of the logic of divine love!

For the contemplative Christian in deeper prayer of heart-speaks-to-heart, the terrifying *kenosis* of self-emptying even to the last drop of blood and water has its fullest meaning only in being an exact *image* of the heart of God the Father. This heart is poured out to us in His infinite, tender, self-sacrificing love for each individual.

This is My Body

It is especially in the Last Supper that Jesus pours out in a heartful confession to His followers the great love He has for them and for His Heavenly Father. He acts out in beautiful, symbolic gestures the love in His heart that would be acted out definitively in the piercing of His heart on the next day.

Now in that upper chamber, alone with His friends, Jesus opens His loving heart to them. It is a humble heart that wants to serve as a slave. He bends down and washes the feet of the disciples. This is an image of God's divine power placed at the service of men. "My Father goes on working, and so do I" (Jn 5:17). This loving service in action is seen in its fullness when Jesus takes bread into His hands, then the cup of wine, and lays Himself out upon the table under the symbols of His death: the separate species of bread and wine. His liturgical symbolism looks to His death and offering of Himself even unto the last drop of blood on the cross.

Can we imagine the depths of love and joy in the heart of Jesus who is able at this moment to give Himself totally to us and to remain ever represented in the Eucharist at the peak of self-giving love? We are shown a flood of newly experienced love in the heart of Jesus for His disciples. Then, through them, He gives Himself for us. He does not merely die for us, but shares in His very being with the Father by giving us His body as food and His blood as drink.

His other powerful miracles and healings have meaning in the light of this greatest power of communication whereby He gives Himself to us in the complete gift as the supreme "Philanthropos." He finds a way to remain among us, imaging always the sacrificing love of the Father. He establishes by that act of self-giving unto blood the New Covenant between God and mankind. Jesus renews the tender, spousal love of Yahweh for His people. This is the marriage feast which Jesus' Father celebrates on His behalf in giving Him to us. Jesus is full of tender love and wishes to give Himself, "to lay down his life for his friends" (Jn 15:13).

Entering into the Heart of Christ

A Christian, who has understood through the Spirit of love the infinite love of Jesus for him/her, will live more and more consciously in the union with Christ as the guiding force. "Think of the love that the Father has lavished on us . . ." (1 Jn 3:1). If Jesus, so full of love for you, truly abides within you, how can you ever again be lonely? Is it difficult for you now to keep in contact with Him in His infinite, ever-now love for you unto death?

No matter how weak you are, when you are aware of such a friend living within you, giving you courage to become one with Him in all that you do and think and say, you can accomplish infinitely more than what you could do alone. ". . . for cut off from me you can do nothing" (Jn 15:5). Peace and joy of the Spirit of Jesus govern all your thoughts, words and deeds because you have experienced the infinite love of God. This love is not very far away, but abides within your very *heart*, your deepest consciousness, through the gifts of the Spirit of faith, hope and love. No force outside can harm you ". . . because you are from God and you have in you one who is greater than anyone in this world" (1 Jn 4:4).

Look at your weaknesses of the past. See that there remains much darkness and sin in your members, as St. Paul writes about himself (Rm 7:23). You are exhorted by the Master to keep close to Him.

Make your home in me, as I make mine in you.
As a branch cannot bear fruit all by itself,

but must remain part of the vine,
neither can you unless you remain in me . . .
Whoever remains in me, with me in him,
bears fruit in plenty;
for cut off from me you can do nothing (Jn 15:4–5).

True Devotion to Christ

True devotion must be more than the experience of how much God loves you through the mirror of that love in Christ Jesus. Love begets love, and obedience out of love is the way love is engendered in your heart. You will wish therefore in each moment to love God willingly through obedience to His holy will. You will seek to render loving obedience to His word spoken within your heart.

One with Christ within you, you move out into your world around you. In loving, obeying abandonment to Christ you seek to live in love in every thought, word and deed. You experience a continued growth in simplicity and freedom that approaches what Jesus Himself experienced as He centered His whole earthly life on doing only the will of His Father. Inordinate attachments and passions are cut out from your life. Constancy and equanimity become the effects of your being rooted in the unchangeable love of God. Your whims and selfish feelings have no power now to determine your attitudes and ways of acting. Now you seek at all times to do only God's will in return for the infinite love He pours into your "heart" through the heart of Jesus. Your devotion to Him in His loving heart is measured by your love toward every man and woman you meet. You stretch out to share with Jesus Christ, the lover of mankind, His great love for the world.

VIII

Mary, Fellow Pilgrim

As you have grown older and wiser, more loving and more prayerful, your loving attitude toward your earthly mother, whether she be still living on this earth or in God's eternal presence, has changed greatly. Is it any wonder that your devotion to Mary, without whom you would not have been birthed into God's eternal life through her Son and our God, Jesus Christ, would change?

Mary, in the ordinariness of her very humble, hidden life, is the archetype of what all human beings are called to be, namely, virgin, emptied of selfishness, totally receptive and actively submissive to God's Word through His Holy Spirit. We answer this call to become the mother of Christ to the world through loving service to others.

It is my desire to share through you the gift of Mary, given to St. John at the foot of the Cross and to all Christians, represented by the Beloved Disciple, with our Protestant brothers and sisters. Under the guidance of the Holy Spirit, we realize that we are all born in Christ through the same Mother, Mary, archetype of the Church and of all of us in Christ.

Devotion to Mary the Contemplative

Have you ever reflected on how your devotion to Mary has undergone changes through your years of Christian living? These changes of attitude between you and your Heavenly Mother reflect to some degree the changes you yourself were undergoing as you struggled to become the unique person God was calling you to be in His Word, Jesus Christ.

As a young child, no doubt, you were devoted to Mary in a way similar to your devotion to your earthly mother. She was the powerful Mother in Heaven to whom you directed your "fiery" petitions for this or that gift. You were always confident that if you said enough rosaries or made enough novenas or lighted enough candles before her statue or picture, you would surely "get" what *you* wanted.

Then, as you grew into the adolescence of your physical, psychic and spiritual development, you related to Mary somewhat differently. You were becoming aware of new powers within your being, powers of intellect, will, and emotions. Your sexual powers were unfolding and, in great confusion, you were constantly asking: "Who am I?" Mary became for you a model of purity. You prayed many a rosary that she would intercede for you to keep you pure. Nuns taught you at this stage of objectivizing the role of Mary in your life as a model of holiness, that you were not to do anything that Mary would not do at a prom!

Then you finally arrived at adulthood. At times you even thought and reacted to others in human, stressful situations with patience, kindness and even love, true, unselfish love. You were moving as Mary did all her life-time under the power of God's Spirit in mystery. You were experiencing Mary as really alive and present in her glorious existence as

an active intercessor. She was an archetype of your own increased individuality, in becoming who you were meant to
be in God's Word.

Human Integration

On this adult level of existence which is seen as a mysterious process of unending growth in self-giving to others
in love, you relate to Mary no longer as an objective, static
example of perfection. Now you are striving with God's grace
to become more and more what she has been becoming so
perfectly all her existence. You have entered into the stage
of integrating all elements that go to realize your full potential as a human being. This can be experienced only in contemplating yourself as a child of God, a sharer in God's own
divine nature by grace.

Today psychology tells us much about our own human
development as fully realized persons, freed of the pre-con-
ditionings that have come to us genetically. These pre-con-
ditionings have also come from the society around us and
our education, as well as our own actions and reactions
whereby we made choices. Carl G. Jung in his book, *Answer
to Job*, insists on the importance of Mary as the archetypal
symbol of the feminine in all human beings. He laments the
fact that Protestantism has rejected devotion to Mary,
thereby losing the feminine appreciation for the interior,
contemplative life, becoming a "masculine" form of Christianity. Jung felt that Catholics through their devotion to Mary
had a better chance to unite the consciousness and the unconscious and attain integration in a better way than
Protestants.

Jung writes:

> But if the individuation process is made conscious,
> consciousness must confront the unconscious and
> a balance between the opposites must be found. As

this is not possible through logic, one is dependent on symbols which make the irrational union of opposites possible . . . Faith is certainly right when it impresses on man's mind and heart how infinitely far away and inaccessible God is; but it also teaches his nearness, his immediate presence, and it is just this nearness which has to be empirically real if it is not to lose all significance . . . The religious need longs for wholeness, and therefore lays hold of the images of wholeness offered by the unconscious, which, independently of the conscious mind, rise up from the depths of our psychic nature (*Answer to Job*).

Modern psychology teaches us that integration into a fully realized human person can come only through a harmonious blending of two inner, psychic principles. Some psychologists define one such principle as the *animus*, the intelligible principle which leads to critical reflection, to control and calculation. The other principle is the *anima*, which brings about relationships, especially in true love, of communion and unity. L. Beirnaert insists that "It is the psyche, the anima, the soul that makes contact with God . . . and that is in a feminine relationship with God."

We become fully realized human beings and therefore true Christians by developing firstly our feminine power of receiving love from God, parents and other loving persons. This develops our contemplative abilities to open ourselves with the totality of our being, to stretch in active receptivity toward the Transcendent God. It is to become what we are: empty receptacles to be filled with God's goodness. It is to receive in our existential poverty the love that God first has for us. Only then can we respond with *animus* power to enflesh love for God into love for neighbor.

Mary, the Perfect Christian

Mary has always been regarded by faithful Christians

from earliest times, not only as the model of perfect Christian living, but as the prototype. She was the example, coming at the very beginning of the new age, of what all of us could and should become when we cooperate with God's grace at each moment of our life, as Mary did. She is the archetype or basic symbol of what the Church should be and what you and I as members of that Church should be. Mary is the Virgin, totally emptied of self-centeredness to be filled with divine life through her obedience to God's Word. But she is also the Mother of God who then, to the degree that she has emptied herself and has been filled by God's Spirit of love to bring forth His Word, responds by giving Christ to the world.

Mary stands for Virgin, *anima*, emptied of self, a womb, dark and filled with promises of what could be, sterility that becomes a fertile desert only in the paradox of death-resurrection. Mary is also Mother of God, *animus*, who, surrendering in complete obedience to God's Spirit, brings forth the Word of God and gives Him to the world through her loving response of service.

Mary becomes the Mother of God only because all her life-time she was the virgin-contemplative who lived in the awesome mystery of God's reality. This reality was within her and around her, in every facet of her existence and in every human situation. Mary heard God's Word and obeyed it. Only in a faith similar to Abraham's was she able to believe that out of her impossible sterility as a virgin, God could bring forth not only life but the Eternal Life, Jesus Christ, the Son of God.

Mary, the Contemplative

As you learn to move into the mystery of contemplating the all-pervasive presence of God in your life, in every moment, you begin to understand how Mary was and is still in process of becoming a contemplative. Mary did not listen to

God's Word coming to her as though for the first time when she heard His message through the Angel Gabriel in the Annunciation. She stored up all these things in her heart, says St. Luke (Lk 2:50). Early in life she contemplated God, working in her life in a similar manner as He had worked in the lives of her ancestors of the Old Testament.

Not only was the holiness of the Old Testament known to Mary in her prayerful contemplation of God's Word but she became that holiness by a continued experience of greater intensity. How beautifully the Psalmist outlines a holiness of the Old Testament that Mary strove to attain as she contemplated the everlasting Yahweh:

> I sought the Lord and He answered me
> and delivered me from all my fears.
> Look to Him that you may be radiant with joy
> and your faces may not blush with shame.
> When the afflicted man called out, the Lord heard
> and from all his distress He saved him.
> The angel of the Lord encamps
> around those who fear Him and delivers them.
> Taste and see how good the Lord is;
> happy the man who takes refuge in Him.
> Fear the Lord, you His holy ones
> for naught is lacking to those who fear Him.
> The great grow poor and hungry;
> but those who seek the Lord want for no good
>   thing.
> The Lord has eyes for the just
> and ears for their cry.
> When the just cry out, the Lord hears them
> and from all their distress He rescues them.
> The Lord is close to the brokenhearted;
> and those who are crushed in spirit he saves
> (Ps 33:4–19).

Mary's greatness is part of God's greatness whereby He becomes weak and humble unto obedience to death out of love for us. Her greatness is seen in her ordinariness for she was total emptiness at all times before God's allness. There is a beautiful scene recorded in Matthew's Gospel (also Mk 6:3) that shows the ordinariness of Mary that must have come out of her contemplation of God's greatness in her life at all times. Jesus had come back to His hometown of Nazareth and was teaching in the synagogue. People were amazed at His wisdom and miraculous powers. Against such visible greatness they asked the question: "This is the carpenter's son surely? Is not his mother the woman called Mary . . .?" (Mt 13:55)

This probably was said as an assertion that anybody born of such an ordinary woman as Mary, could not be very important. They had known her in their village as a woman not endowed with extraordinary and powerful gifts. Yet Mary could only contemplate the greatness of the Lord, He who is mighty, who was doing such great things within her and through her for the world. She had to burst out in St. Luke's understanding of her contemplative union with God in utter submission to exclaim: "He who is mighty has done great things for me and holy is his name" (Lk 1:49). Before she could have verbalized the beautiful words of her Magnificat, Mary had to have contemplated these truths deeply within herself over long years of prayerful experiences. "Holy is his name, and his mercy reaches from age to age for those who fear him. He has shown the power of his arm, he has routed the proud of heart. He has pulled down princes from their thrones and exalted the lowly. The hungry he has filled with good things, the rich sent empty away" (Lk 1:46–53).

And before she could run in haste to serve her pregnant cousin, Elisabeth, she had had to be concerned in loving service to others earlier in her life. Mary surrendered in prayer moments and also in her active work to God's will and providential designs working throughout her life. She knew from contemplative experience what St. Paul wrote: "We know that by turning everything to their good God co-operates with all those who love him, with all those that he has called according to his purpose" (Rm 8:28).

Ordinary and Human

A contemplative should be the most ordinary human person, as Jesus and Mary show us. It was in the hiddenness of the thirty years of Nazareth that Jesus, Mary and Joseph became contemplatives in the ordinary circumstances of their lives. In the humdrum details of living in a remote village in Galilee Mary experienced God as penetrating every fiber of her being with His uncreated energies of love. She gave her *fiat* at each moment of her life that would prepare for her fiat in the Annunciation and her fiat at the foot of the cross. Her holiness was a process of continuously discovering God's loving presence in the gift of the moment.

From the inner presence of the spirit, Mary moved freely through life's events and circumstances to respond fully according to the Heavenly Father's mind. "My soul proclaims the greatness of the Lord and my spirit exults in God my saviour . . ." (Lk 1:46). Her life, made up of each moment and her free choices within that moment, brought her into a growing experience, that in all things she was rooted in God's Word, one with the Mind of the Father. Freed from sin and self-seeking, Mary lived in a process of continuous inner attention and vigilance to bring every thought, feeling and deed under God's dominion. Thus she was free to be loved infinitely by her Father and to strive to respond joyfully in a return of that love.

Whether she was carrying water from the village fountain, washing clothes, cleaning her kitchen or visiting a sick neighbor, Mary found the Father's loving presence and praised Him with joyful surrender. She was free to be most human in the most ordinary circumstances of her life. With joyful exuberance Mary could embrace all creatures and use them properly according to her Father's mind. Especially she contemplated God's gentle presence as love in the gifts of the intimate friends God gave her.

As she moved toward a deeper human love for her husband, Joseph, she learned to discover more of God's loveliness in Joseph. His strength and gentleness gave to her a "holy" revelation of God unobtainable in any other way. She found God's love in his pure love and self-sacrifice for her. The New Testament hides her contemplative spirit as she met God in the beauty of her son, Jesus. What human words could ever have expressed the intimacy between her and Jesus in the silence of being in union with each other in total self-surrender!

"Happy the pure in heart; they shall see God" (Mt 5:8). This earth has never seen a vessel as pure as Mary. We can say that we will never see a more "human" person than Mary. She is the true contemplative since she saw reality as closely as God sees it. God infused into her a purified vision that permitted Mary to see the "insideness" of God's presence. She reverenced that presence and humbly strove to serve God's will in each circumstance.

How exciting and more realistic it is to see that Mary's having been conceived immaculately is what true contemplation is all about. She was at each moment being baptized in the Spirit of love and set more and more free to surrender in a corresponding call to live in love as she obeyed the will of the Father. Freedom for her was to be the person God made her to be. "Now this Lord is the Spirit and where the Spirit of the Lord is, there is freedom" (2 Co 3:17). The Spirit within her gave her a new, inner law that freed her from any formalized extrinsicism.

She received her greatness and holiness through a freedom that the Holy Spirit gave her in a continued growth process that was first radicated in His gift of faith. In this faith, Mary assented to God's plan of salvation as taught in the Old Testament. She received in faith the new message of God that the Messiah was coming and she was to be His mother. She responded in faith to the love of God by her complete surrender to serve Him in all things. ". . . because he has looked upon his lowly handmaid" (Lk 1:47).

Her contemplative spirit grew in the strong hope that with God all things are possible. God could do whatever He wished with her. She would hope for a greater fulfillment of

God's glory even though she already had experienced a great share in that glory.

Conceived in Love

Mary's contemplative union with God and her holiness are measured and described in terms of love that grew in her out of the Spirit's faith and hope operating within her at each moment of her life. Mary was freed to love. She freely placed herself in loving service to God's Word, an inner presence of God's love incarnated and living within her. As she received in prayer experiences God's love calling her to participate in a return of love, Mary became progressively more free to love others by seeking to serve them.

She experienced always the paradox that to be free is to become a slave to serve others in love. Mary knew that she was called to serve others in love. She lived this love as the privilege of giving herself to another in service, as God has continuously done with His people. We will miss the true, ultimate meaning of contemplation if we miss this aspect of Mary's life as summarized by St. Paul:

> You were called, as you know, to liberty; but be careful, or this liberty will provide an opening for self-indulgence. Serve one another, rather, in works of love, since the whole of the Law is summarized in a single command: Love your neighbor as yourself (Ga 5:13–14).

Mary loves because each day she progressively becomes more aware of how beautiful she is and how completely she is loved by her Heavenly Father through His Word. No wonder she could boast in being God's masterpiece and humbly confess that God had made her great. "Yes, from this day forward all generations will call me blessed, for the Almighty has done great things for me. Holy is his name" (Lk 1:48–49).

Yet her love demanded a constant cooperation with God's uncreated energies of love, His grace, given in each moment of each human situation. All too often we perhaps pictured Mary as perfectly sanctified in the womb of her mother, conceived without sin, so that she never really had to grow as Jesus Himself did in wisdom and knowledge and grace before God and man (Lk 2:52). If Jesus had been tempted in all things and yet never sinned (Heb 4:15), we can easily enough believe that Mary had to cooperate. This had to be a constant struggle in faith, hope and love. Vatican II brings this point out clearly in showing that Mary's personal act of faith, hope and love and her cooperation continuously with the Holy Spirit were in a process of growth in grace. Mary is our archetype and that of the Church because she is the perfect pilgrim, "homo viator," who contemplates by faith and obedience, hope and burning love, the saving work of God. (*Lumen Gentium*; #58).

Her experience of God's infinite love for her and for His people makes it possible for her to give of that love. Ultimately Mary is the contemplative and archetype of all of us in her virginal emptiness and active receptivity because she shares with others the riches she has experienced. From feminine to masculine, from *anima* to *animus*, from a womb that receives rich life and opens to release that life, so Mary becomes for us the completely realized, integrated human being. She is the contemplative in action, the virgin-mother of the Word of God, receiving and sharing that Divine Life with the whole world.

IX

Sunrise: Christ is Risen

The celebration of the Resurrection of Jesus Christ ushers us into a new time and a new space. It is a sharing in the now eternity of the Risen Jesus, as we surrender to His indwelling Presence. This new time of the Risen Christ intersects our old, broken time and becomes a transforming leaven changing our historical time into salvific time. Our old time is not destroyed and done away with but it becomes transformed from within the very historicity of our given human situation. It is a gradual consummation of time through the presence of the Risen Lord inserted into the very broken materiality of the universe.

Contemplation begins when we break through the objectivity of our historical, linear perspective in our *now* time in the space of our heart where the triune God dwells within us. So few Christians ever make the passage from a prayer form of "talking" to Jesus as an object, to the more contemplative type of prayer as presence that is the work of the

Holy Spirit. It is the Holy Spirit who prays within us when we surrender all our thoughts, images, feelings and varied ways of keeping God at arm's length. Contemplation is our participation in a conscious manner given us by the Spirit through increasing faith, hope and love in the triune God. This life is an eternal happening taking place always within our "heart." Such a contemplative experience of community as God's personalized presence, Father, Son and Holy Spirit, becomes ever more real to us, while it transforms our lives and our views of the real world. The resurrection of Jesus Christ is the breakthrough into that experience of the triune God as saving community.

Contemplation and Jesus Risen

If you wish to test the level of prayer on which you habitually move to make contact with the hidden God, test it with your approach to the basic dogma around which Christianity revolves, namely, the resurrection of Christ Jesus. There is one approach both to prayer and doctrines which is a man-centered activity involving much thought. We could call this meditation, or discursive prayer.

There is also another, more advanced approach which is the entrance into the world of non-objectivity, of mystery, in which we meet God by falling down and worshiping Him, the Burning Bush, without any of our own controlled securities holding God "over there." The 14th century anonymous English author of *The Cloud of Unknowing* describes this way of prayer as touching God by love, not thought. "By love He may be touched and embraced, never by thought."

The early Fathers of the Church feared the formulation of dogmas, since that tended to reduce the living faith of the Gospels to a "system of thought." St. Hilary of Poitiers, a Father of the Latin Church, wrote in the fourth century that which was held universally among the Greek Fathers:

The guilt of the heretics and blasphemers compels us to undertake what is unlawful, to scale arduous heights, to speak of the ineffable, and to trespass upon forbidden places. And since by faith alone we should fulfill what is commanded, namely, to adore the Father, to venerate the Son with Him, and to abound in the Holy Spirit, we are forced to raise our lowly words to subjects which cannot be described. By the guilt of another we are forced into guilt, so that what should have been restricted to the pious contemplation of our minds is now exposed to the dangers of human speech.

Experiencing the Mystery

Anyone who has participated in the Easter services in a Byzantine church understands the radical difference of approach to the Risen Christ from that of Western churches. With the church at midnight in complete darkness and the setting of Calvary still standing in the middle of the church banked with flowers, the priest walks through the church with a candle, the Gospel book and an icon of the Resurrection. Outside he knocks on the closed door and then sings with joyful triumph: "Christ is risen. . . ." As he and all the people following him enter with lighted candles, they shout the refrain: "Christ is risen! He is truly risen!" One experiences the new victory of Christ over death. We find it easier to believe also that the same "divinizing" process has already begun in our lives and in those praying around us.

We could learn much from Eastern Christians who teach us how to move into an experience of mystery in contemplative prayer. For such Christians the icon of the Resurrection is not an objectivized picture of the historical Jesus coming out of the tomb, with the soldiers falling to the earth in terror. Jesus, with all the saints standing in the background, is seen pulling an aged man out of the bowels of the earth.

Easter is joy in the new act of God who is *now* restoring man to new life in Him. A new creation has begun, not only of the Risen Jesus, but of human beings sharing in His new life and of the whole cosmos transfigured by His glorious presence.

Through liturgical and biblical revival, Western Christianity is recapturing the intimate connection between Good Friday and Easter, between Christ's sufferings and death and His entrance into His glorification. Both Roman Catholics and Protestants had been too absorbed for many centuries in an *atonement* theology that sprang chiefly from St. Anselm's speculations. When Jesus died on the cross and paid back our debt to the Father, there was little importance assigned to His resurrection in the history of man's redemption.

In theology manuals it was like an afterthought: "Oh, yes, and then what happened to Jesus was that He rose from the dead and ascended to Heaven where He now sits in glory before He comes back to us again in judgment." Our prayer over the mysteries of Easter usually consisted in a joyful congratulating of Jesus, that He who suffered for us is now glorified and will never have to suffer again. We go through each detail of His resurrectional apparitions to His followers as we make acts of faith that He is God since only God, as He promised, could raise Himself from the dead.

A New Time

But the New Testament gives us a different vision of the resurrection. It cannot be separated from Jesus' suffering and death, nor can it be separated from our new history in a life in the Risen Christ. The early Christian believers rejoiced in Christ's resurrection because of the saving power, not only of His death on the cross, but also because of His new glorious life. St. Peter writes:

Blessed be God the Father of our Lord Jesus Christ,
who in his great mercy has given us a new birth as

his sons, by raising Jesus Christ from the dead, so that we have a sure hope and the promise of an inheritance that can never be spoilt or soiled and never fade away, because it is being kept for you in the heavens (1 P 1:3-4).

God has brought Jesus back from the dead "to become the great Shepherd of the sheep by the blood that sealed an eternal covenant . . ." (Heb 13:20). Joy is everywhere evident in the New Testament because Jesus has gone forward into a completely new existence which He now makes possible to share with His followers. "I was dead and now I am to live forever and ever, and I hold the keys of death and of the underworld" (Rv 1:18).

The role of Christ's resurrection in our redemption is more clearly stated by St. Paul. ". . . Jesus who was put to death for our sins and raised to life to justify us" (Rm 4:25). Jesus "died and was raised to life" (2 Co 5:15) for us that we might have eternal life. In St. Paul's classical text showing how Christ's resurrection is part of our salvation from sins, he writes: ". . . and if Christ has not been raised, you are still in your sins" (1 Co 15:17).

St. Paul prays for the knowledge of Jesus Risen, which should also be our desire to experience in prayer, as a gift from God beyond anything our reasoning powers could arrive at:

> All I want is to know Christ and the power of his resurrection and to share his sufferings by reproducing the pattern of his death. That is the way I can hope to take my place in the resurrection of the dead (Ph 3:10-11).

Christ's resurrection cannot be studied solely from the account in the New Testament of His resurrection and apparitions. The New Testament accounts are witnesses to the resurrection and glorification of Jesus of Nazareth by men and women who met the historical Jesus in events that were rooted in a faith experience. Jesus risen was able to send them His vivifying Spirit, who could lead them into the *now* experience of Jesus raising them beyond sin and death into a share of His resurrection and eternal life.

The actual happening of Jesus' resurrection was not witnessed by anyone. It could not have been so since it happened not in our historical time (*chronos* in Greek). Jesus is inserted into human history through the resurrection by means of being a new creation, a new beginning, that shatters all historical categories. This new time is the historical reality of Christ's new resurrectional creation that allows us also to live the eschatological future, the *kairos* time of eternal salvation.

Only those who were opened to the presence of Jesus were able, not only to "see" Him as risen, but were also able to experience His glory and know that they were sharing in that same glory. Jesus could not be seen by those who did not believe in Him. He was not "observable" in human form any longer as He was before His death. Then He was still one with a sinful world. He had laid aside His glory in becoming one with the sinful world. But now, "God raised this man Jesus to life and all of us are witnesses to that" (Ac 2:32).

A New Presence

Did you ever wonder whether the Apostles missed the old Jesus? We never learn of their yearning in a nostalgia for the past "good old days." They are not seen after the resurrection of Jesus wanting to contact Him as He existed earlier. For they had experienced through the outpouring of the Holy Spirit an evolution in Jesus. He had progressed forward. Not only did the Father exalt Him in glory and place Him at His right hand, but Jesus was now present to His disciples in a new and more involving way. No longer was Jesus physically present to them as before in one limited place in Palestine. But the disciples of Jesus discovered that He was, in

His glorification, now declared the living, eternal presence of God's love for each human being in all times. Jesus is now Lord of the universe and God of all.

Still Jesus did condescend to accommodate Himself to His disciples. He took upon Himself a form or various forms of physical presence to them so that with a material body He was able to be seen, to speak, to eat and to be touched by them and to carry the wounds of His passion. To meet Jesus as the New Creation, the disciples needed to make the step gradually from the historical Jesus to the risen Jesus. Thus those eye-witnesses had a direct and personal experience of a "bodied" Jesus. It was because they did, that successive generations of Christian believers, including you and me of the 20th century, could be brought into a "faithful" experience of the existence of Jesus in glory, living within them in the most immanent union as Vine and branches.

This new presence of Jesus Risen makes the contemplative life possible for us. The Church gives us this message in various apparitions of Jesus to His early disciples. Mary Magdalen is told, and the early Christian community is telling its members: "Do not cling to me as you formerly knew and loved me . . . Go and find the brethren and there you will also discover me in the only way I wish to be present to you" (cf.: Jn 20:17). The message of the Church is: "Happy are those who have not seen and yet believe" (Jn 20:29). To the disciples at Emmaus Jesus is discovered in the breaking of the bread and in the Christian community (Lk 24:15 ff.).

We Can Share in Christ's Victory

Jesus Risen is glorified by the Father and is now becoming the Lord of the universe by raising us up into a new creation. "Anyone who is in Christ, he is a new creation; the old creation has gone, and now the new one is here . . ." (2 Co 5:17 ff.) Jesus Risen exerts a universal and absolute power and dominion over all creatures. ". . . now he has reconciled you by his death and in that mortal body. Now you are able to appear before him holy, pure and blameless as long as you persevere and stand firm on the solid base of the faith" (Col 1:22–23).

Jesus' victory over sin and death can be seen only in His members as we accept the good news of His victory. We allow Him, through His Holy Spirit, to enter into His glorious, eternal life by the forgiveness of our sins and sharing in God's divine life. Jesus in His risen humanity is the first fruit of the new creation, the new Adam and He holds out to all of us a rebirth unto new life through His Holy Spirit. . . . "He saved us, by means of the cleansing water of rebirth and by renewing us with the Holy Spirit which He has so generously poured over us through Jesus Christ our Savior . . . to become heirs looking forward to inheriting eternal life" (Ti 3:5–7).

The victory that you and I can share in as we contemplate the Risen Jesus living within us, brings us the knowledge of the Father and Jesus His Son through the Holy Spirit. It is a knowledge that brings eternal life and a share even now in the resurrection of Jesus (Jn 17:3). This knowledge is received in prayer and is experienced every time you live in self-sacrificing love for another person, knowing the infinite love of God in Jesus that drove Him to empty Himself. In dying for you unto the last drop of blood, He imaged the perfect love of the Heavenly Father for you.

Only when Jesus died and was risen to a new oneness in human form of imaging the love of the Father for each of us, could He pour into our hearts the Father's Spirit of love:

> . . . the Spirit of God has made his home in you. . . . Though your body may be dead it is because of sin, but if Christ is in you then your spirit is life itself because you have been justified: and if the Spirit of him who raised Jesus from the dead is living in you, then he who raised Jesus from the dead will give life to your own mortal bodies through his Spirit living in you (Rm 8:9–11).

A Now Resurrection

Through the Spirit of the Risen Jesus living in you, you are made an heir with Christ. As you share in His sufferings so you also will share in His glory (Rm 8:16–17; Ga 4:6–7). Now hopefully you and I can break away from viewing our resurrection as an objectified event at the last moment of this world's material existence.

As you meet the Risen Jesus in the new space of what Scripture calls your "heart", there in faith, hope and love you begin to experience your true self in being "in Christ Jesus." In the space of your heart, in the deepest reaches of your consciousness you encounter the risen Jesus in the spaceless space of His healing love.

You receive eternal life in the space of your oneness with the Risen Lord. This new life in Christ has been yours in Baptism. It grows each time you "put on Christ" by dying to selfishness and rising to a new oneness in Him. The church becomes the "space" where you can encounter Jesus and grow into a greater oneness with Him risen in the sacraments, especially in the "breaking of the Bread." In the Eucharist you meet the new presence of the Risen Jesus that goes beyond His physical presence and yet is also spatially found within the confines of the materiality of bread and wine and the Christian community, the Body of Christ.

Jesus' risen presence is also present in His Word as it is preached within the Body, the Church. He becomes present in His Word as it is taught by the Church through its hierarchical authority with its charism to build up the Body in truth and love.

Contemplating the Indwelling Presence

But Jesus' indwelling presence within you, in the depths of your heart, is what makes it possible now for you to be always present to Him and Him to you. Love grows most when there is immediacy. Now "by the game of the resurrection," in the words of Teilhard de Chardin, God has pitched His tent forever through the glorified humanity of Jesus Risen.

The work of the risen Lord is to release His Spirit within your heart. The Spirit reveals to you continually that the Trinity of Father, Son and Holy Spirit dwells within you. "Didn't you realize that you were God's temple and that the Spirit of God was living among you? . . . the temple of God is sacred; and you are that temple" (1 Co 3:16-17). That Spirit is raising you to higher levels of awareness of God's intimate presence to you and by pouring faith, hope and love into you, the Spirit makes it possible for you to be continually present to God at all times. This is the goal of the contemplative life: to live in God's reality at all times and to surrender in loving obedience to His uncreated energies of love.

The Risen Lord floods you from within with His transfiguring light. As you learn to surrender to His resurrectional presence living within you, you grow daily into greater transformation and oneness with the Lord Jesus. You move away from the darkness of selfishness to the loving light of Christ who gradually permeates your body, soul and spirit relationships in all your thoughts, words and deeds.

As you allow the Risen Jesus to take over in your life and you are guided by His inner light, your thoughts become centered constantly upon God.

> Let your thoughts be on heavenly things, not on the things that are on the earth, because you have died, and now the life you have is hidden with Christ in God. But when Christ is revealed—and he is your life—you too will be revealed in all your glory with him (Col 3:2-4).

But you also are gifted in such a contemplative prayer by the Spirit of Jesus Risen, to discover the same indwelling light of Christ and His resurrectional presence shining "diaphanously" throughout the entire material creation. You are able to contemplate the physical world around you in the light of Christ's resurrectional power that raises up all things to a new sharing in His divine life.

Releasing the Risen Jesus

To the degree that you become aware of being in the risen Christ . . . to that degree Jesus Risen will begin to operate in and through you to extend His Kingdom, His reign of love, to other human beings. Christ is the Head and is present to you by His filling activity. He is operating from within you with His infinite power, but He depends upon your readiness to allow His creative love to flow through you outwardly to others. "Each one of us, however, has been given his own share of grace, given as Christ allotted it" (Ep 4:7).

He lives in you and me in different and unique ways. He manifests these diverse ways through the charisms that His Spirit of love gives us. These innumerable charisms or gifts are all given to aid in the building up of the Body of Christ that is His Church (cf.: Co 12:4–11). What a challenge it is for us to break from the concept of praying to a Risen Jesus, seated in Heaven in glory, and to discover that presence of the Risen Lord living within us . . . waiting to release His conquering, transforming power from within us in the context of our daily situations.

How humbling it is to contemplate that Jesus' resurrection will not be revealed in all its glory unless you and I discover that transforming power living within us and surrender at each moment to His presence of love. ". . . You are from God and you have in you one who is greater than anyone in this world" (1 Jn 4:4). We know our poverty and we offer it to the Risen Lord. He alone can make us not only want Him but He can also supply all that is necessary to spread the good news that we have seen the Lord and He is risen indeed! Then the prayer of the Byzantine Church that is sung with such exultation all through the Easter season until Ascension Thursday, will become our contemplative experience also: "Christ is risen from the dead, trampling down death by death and granting life to those who are in the tomb."

X

Sunset: Walk into Glory

The annual liturgical season of Lent calls us into the desert of our heart to give special attention to the *not-yet* areas of our human development. The Easter cycle highlights the *already*, transforming presence of Jesus risen and glorified, as He releases His Spirit so we can, even now, share in His eternal life. How important it is for all of us Christians to confront the sin and brokenness in ourselves. It is the first step in a constant conversion process, before we can seriously surrender our lives in total humble dependency upon God as our Ultimate Source of Life.

The first element of the desert experience is to enter into the darkness of sin and all other obstacles that prevent us from becoming the persons God wishes us to be. Let us look at three areas of so-called obstacles that can, if we allow them to happen, become destructive elements preventing the paschal victory of Christ from becoming transformative in our lives.

The Mid-Life Desert

I am sure that you who are reading this have become aware of much recent writing dealing with adult life-cycles. Drs. Erick Erickson, Kohlberg and Piaget are psychologists who give us either physical-psychosocial or faith dimensions of human growth from infancy to old age. What is important about their proposed stages of human development is that these authors highlight human development as a continued process, as a pilgrimage toward an ever-deepening spiritual reality. This reality demands our self-knowledge of what is happening and our cooperation to move our lives into greater mystery, joy, salvation, creative suffering, faith, hope and love.

Let us look at three levels of human growth that most of us probably are now passing through, or, by God's grace, will soon confront. The first major challenge toward integration or disintegration comes during mid-life adulthood.

This is the time, according to Dr. William Kraft, between the ages of 39 to 49. It is a great threshold where, after the busyness and accomplishments of young adulthood, we stand back and ask, "Who am I beyond the things I do?" "Am I not more than a housewife with a role defined by certain work responsibilities?" If I am a teacher, I may ask: "Is this the function that makes me be *me*?" "Where is my life going by way of deeper meaningfulness? What does it mean to live a fully human and meaningful life?"

One response to the desert of crisis of limits can be similar to that of the Israelites in the Sinai Desert. Some wanted to "regress," i.e. to run back to a lower level of responsible living, back to the "flesh pots" of Egypt. Some mid-lifers may immerse themselves in more busyness and hyperactivity.

They may seek escape by inordinate attachments to sense pleasures of food, drink, sex, travel or anything else that diverts them from facing the crisis of mid-life.

Surrender is the Key

Men, especially, (and also women of a strongly developed *animus* nature) are vulnerable to depression. They are forced to face their helplessness as they are called to confront their unfulfilled lives. Death leers at us as it taunts us with our weaknesses and failures.

How are we to respond to such a crisis in our lives? Just as the Israelites in the desert were challenged by Yahweh to break their idols and make Him their sole support, so too are we called to take a new leap in faith. Beyond death is there eternal life? Beyond the limits of our finiteness can we really surrender to God?

Amidst the mounting trials and tribulations that creep out from within our personal consciousness and our unconscious, everything seems so dark! The desert is dry and empty. Where is God? With St. John of the Cross, we lament in our contemplative prayer:

> Where have You hidden,
> Beloved, and left me moaning?
> You fled like the stag
> after wounding me;
> I went out calling You, and You were gone.
> (*Spiritual Canticle*)

Will we yield to pride or despondency, to a *macho* attack of *animus* or a weak *anima* whimper of "does anyone care"? Light has been eclipsed; the way seems uncertain. In spiritual boredom we feel suffocated by immobility, confined and blocked at every turn. We cry out to God for His infinite mercy, yet think that there is no one to hear our cry. In such inner poverty, we are challenged to believe with new earnestness in our Creator. We search for the presence of God as the only source of reality. God is finally becoming God!

St. Isaac the Syrian of the 7th century describes such interior trials that may come to us during the crisis of our limits:

> Trials which God allows to attack men who puff themselves up in the face of God's goodness and who offend him by their pride, are the following: withdrawal of the force of wisdom which men possess, constant presence of a lustful thought which gives them no peace, and which is allowed in them to curb their conceit; quick temper; desire to have everything their own way, to argue, to reprimand others; a heart that despises everyone; a mind gone completely astray; blasphemy against the name of God; absurd and laughable suspicions that they are scorned by people, deprived of the honor due to them, that demons mock them and put them to shame, both openly and secretly by every kind of means; and finally, the desire to be in touch with the world and circulate in it, to talk endlessly and chatter senselessly, to be always in search of news and even of false prophecies, to promise much that is beyond their strength. These are spiritual trials.

How are we to handle such a state in which we find ourselves? The remedy is always humility of heart which purifies our pride and spirit of independence. We are being called to faith in prayer and in the context of our daily living, to abandon ourselves totally to God's love. We must enter into the inner battle alone and remain there in a state of deep abandonment, cost what it may in personal agony. Only by a compelete self-abandonment to the mercy of God, can we stifle and repel the desire to be free from such sufferings. Then we can abandon ourselves completely to whatever God sends, even if it should be greater suffering. We must "stay in our cell," that is, remain in our heart, where the Light of

Christ shines to dissipate the darkness.

St. Paul's advice will be a guideline and a source of consolation: "You can trust God not to let you be tried beyond your strength, and with any trial he will give you a way out of it and the strength to bear it" (1 Co 10:13). Isaiah the prophet also exhorts the people of God to trust in God through all darkness:

Let anyone who fears Yahweh among you
listen to the voice of his servant!
Whoever walks in darkness,
and has no light shining for him,
let him trust in the name of Yahweh,
let him lean on his God (Is 50:10).

We are called to surrender totally to God as the Ultimate in our lives. When we humbly accept our limitations and do so even with some joy and excitement, we find a mellowing of our impetuous nature. This shows itself in our ability to accept the limitations of others and excuse their failings. We become filled with a motherly compassionate love and mercy toward all others, especially those who fall as we ourselves have fallen.

Middle-Aged Adulthood

Middle age is the period of our life when we reach the mark of a half century. In our fifties there is a greater power of death asserting itself than in any previous stage of our development. This comes through the increased losses we have to suffer in terms of our own bodily sufferings and the physical loss of loved ones and friends through death. We experience setbacks, as younger persons replace us in the production line of work, etc.

Simone Weil, the French Jewess, died from a hunger fast for those suffering in German concentration camps in World

War II. She describes this state of affliction when God's presence is solid, dark absence:

> Affliction makes God appear to be absent for a time, more absent than a dead man, more absent than light in the utter darkness of a cell. A kind of horror submerges the whole soul. During this absence there is nothing to love, the soul ceases to love, God's absence becomes final. The soul has to go on loving in the emptiness (aimer a vide) or at least to go on wanting to love, though it may only be with an infinitesimal part of itself. Then, one day, God will come to show himself to this soul and to reveal the beauty of the world to it, as in the case of Job. (Essay: "The Love of God and Affliction")

This stage of our life brings us into the last struggle before we resign ourselves to old age. It is a tension between feeling still "alive" and yet smelling death all around us in relationship to God, self and neighbor. This terrifying inner psychic and spiritual tension seems not to have any external cause which would explain the void effect so consistently felt day and night. We are called to realize what true creaturely poverty of spirit means as an entrance ticket to the Kingdom of Heaven.

Sense of Sin

Such an experience of our existential "void" brings with it a new sense of sin. It moves us beyond a sense of guilt that we may have had at an earlier stage of our religious development. Now sin brings us into a sense of violating our own authenticity, by being deliberately false to our innermost being. Sin takes on the aspect of an inescapable inner cancer, a radical evil and sickness in our spirit and we become aware that we alone are the ones responsible. We have turned against God in the deepest reaches of our spirits and now we desperately want to clutch Him. But He seems so far away. He seems to have abandoned us. Where can we turn to find health for our sick spirits?

No longer do we feel that in the area of *doing*, we have done wrong, but that we are *wrong*, worthless, false persons. We relate to Job in his stripped condition as he sits on the dung heap considering the vanity of everything. Yet we seem to be even poorer than Job was. Such inner evils are magnified on a world-wide scale, in a way Job could never have experienced. We feel responsibility for lighting the furnaces of Auschwitz and for dropping the big bomb on Nagasaki and Hiroshima. *The Day After* is our responsibility. We cry out in utter helplessness: "From the depths I call to you, Yahweh, Lord, listen to my cry for help!" (Ps 130:1). And His answer is: Silence.

A Time of Reconciliation and Integration

In this important silent desert of our lives much can happen in our spiritual life. We move away from being centered upon ourselves as the pivot of all reality. Stretching out for God's forgiving and merciful love, we develop an *anima* relationship of lovingly listening to God and to others around us on deeper levels of dialogue. Our spiritual dimension is being integrated into physical and psychological dimensions. We are called to accept more profoundly than at any other previous time of our spiritual development, our radical dependency and complete abandonment to God.

A mellowness comes over us as we accept all that happens to us with a peace and joy. We begin to believe that, really, all things work unto good for those who love the Lord (Rm 8:28). Wisdom we never manifested before in dealing with problems of others shines through to their astonishment in our new-founded maturity.

And yet what is happening is the beginning of the harvest of what was planted and cultivated so many years earlier. We reap anew, filling what recently had only been a seemingly void, spiritual crater.

However, being in the middle-age crisis does not mean that all of us will automatically reap the harvest. The call and challenge are there. We can respond negatively by turning away from the conflict. We can seek consolation and pleasures in things and persons as little saviors. By staying in the dark desert we are crying out for God's help! If we make an effective resolve to discipline ourselves from all inordinate attachments to anybody or anything but God, we can experience the wisdom of God's Spirit leading us into an inner world of values hitherto not understood. These values embraced, are essential to our meaningfulness.

The Home-Stretch

The last years of our life stretch from the mid-60's to our earthly death. These are our "elderly" years and they bring with them their special challenges and a call to greater spiritual growth. Many of the problems of the elderly in the western world stem from a materialistic culture. It places its greatest value on what people produce, or do, and not on their individual worth.

Old age can be the beginning of a hell if we refuse to face the challenge of our imminent physical death. To give it ultimate meaning, we need a deepening faith in God's eternal life already given to us to lead us *home,* into a greater sharing of true life in Him.

At such an age level, with the lack of physical health and social acceptance, we are being called by God to go deeper into our desert to intensify our faith in Him alone. He is our supreme and ultimate source of all happiness. Retirement from work and the usual routine of our earlier life can provide us with time to be the persons we wanted to be. We no longer put off answering the question: What is my life's ultimate meaning?

Hope in Darkness

If old age unfolds as a culmination of all other levels of development, then it can bring us through darkness into a deeper hope in everlasting life. We are faced with the realization that we are on the last leg of a long journey. The end may come around the next bend in the road. But Christian hope can flood us with a childlike, pure trust in the loving Father. Such a hope, expressed before others younger than we are in a life to come, can become our greatest witness to Christ as the Life and Resurrection (Jn 11:25–26).

We have the opportunity to live out our faith, hope and love of God, by living each moment with joyful excitement. We stretch out in peace toward Heaven as our eternal home. The full maturity of the seed has ripened into the realized fruit, ready to be plucked in a glorious harvest and homecoming.

Life cannot be lived without the good news of Easter. As you honestly confront the demonic forces lurking deep within the desert of your heart, you realize also that there is a partial acceptance of the *already*. You experience, even now, that Jesus has risen and shares His new life with you, in some limited way. Yet no one can carry you through your own desert. No one can live your life for you. Only you can stretch out in darkness to discover what it means to see that darkness transformed. Darkness becomes meaningful light as you surrender to Christ, your Spouse, your Lord and Master, your God and Savior.

JOURNEY INTO CONTEMPLATION   3.95

George A. Maloney, S.J. This book is an in-depth handbook of guidance, inspiration and concrete advice. In it, Father Maloney provides sure teachings on deep union with God, discussing techniques, problems and anticipated rewards. Small groups who pray together contemplatively are also counseled. The author is a master retreat director and writer of many books, including our *The Returning Sun.*

RECONCILIATION:
The Sacramental Path to Peace   5.95

Msgr. David E. Rosage. Many of life's problems stem from strained or fragmented interpersonal relationships caused by anger, pride, jealousy, self-centeredness, etc. We may not readily recognize these causes since we have lost our sense of sin. In this book we gain insight into the merciful heart of Jesus which leads us to appreciate more fully the Sacrament of Penance as a channel of forgiveness and healing and peace.

FINDING PEACE IN PAIN
The Reflections of a Christian
Psychotherapist   3.50

Yvonne C. Hebert, M.A., M.F.C.C. This book offers a positive approach to overcome the paralyzing effects of emotional hurt in difficult life situations which can't be avoided or changed. Each of the ten chapters clearly illustrates how this form of special prayer can transform life's hurts into opportunities for emotional and spiritual growth. Ms. Hebert draws the reader into the real-life situations of those whom she counsels to join their pain to the sufferings of Christ in His Passion.

THIRSTING FOR GOD
IN SCRIPTURE   2.95

James McCaffrey, D.C.D. In this book, the author directs our attention to the Bible as a means of slaking that thirst, as a true source of light for the searching mind and heart. Several texts of scripture are quoted at length and discussed. The copious references from other texts, not quoted, enable the reader to compare and contrast for him/herself the ways of the Spirit. It is by reading the Bible text itself that the truth and comfort of God's word may sink into our lives.

PRAYING WITH MARY   3.50

Msgr. David E. Rosage. This handy little volume offers twenty-four short meditations or contemplations on the key events in the life of our Blessed Mother. The presentation is short, simple and to the point. The object is to turn the user to the New Testament so that he or she can bask in the light of God's Word, grow in love of that Word and respond to it as fully as possible. For a growing insight into Mary's interior life, these short reflections can be very helpful. *Reign of the Sacred Heart*

SPIRITUAL DIRECTION
Contemporary Readings   5.95

Edited by Kevin Culligan, O.C.D. The revitalized ministry of spiritual direction is one of the surest signs of renewal in today's Church. In this book seventeen leading writers and spiritual directors discuss history, meaning, demands and practice of this ministry. Readers of the book should include not just a spiritual elite, but the entire Church — men and women, clergy and laity, members of religious communities.

ENCOUNTERING THE LORD
IN DAILY LIFE   4.50

Msgr. David E. Rosage. Delightfully spiced with humor and full of wisdom, this book is intended for all who would like to follow St. Paul's admonition to "pray constantly" but who "don't have time." The author helps us turn the mundane actions of life—sipping a cup of coffee, the exhilaration of jogging or the anonymity of an elevator ride—into food for prayer. The book also has quotations from Scripture which focus on the chapter and can carry through to our daily lives.

THE RETURNING SUN
Hope for a Broken World   2.50

George A. Maloney, S.J. In this collection of meditations, the author draws on his own experiences rooted in Eastern Christianity to aid the reader to enter into the world of the "heart." It is hoped that through contemplation of this material he/she will discover the return of the inextinguishable Sun of the universe, Jesus Christ, in a new and more experiential way.

BREAD FOR THE EATING   3.50

Kelly B. Kelly. Sequel to the popular *Grains of Wheat,* this small book of words received in prayer draws the reader closer to God through the imagery of wheat being processed into bread. The author shares her love of the natural world.

LIVING HERE AND HEREAFTER
Christian Dying,
Death and Resurrection   2.95

Msgr. David E. Rosage. The author offers great comfort to us by dispelling our fears and anxieties about our life after this earthly sojourn. Based on God's Word as presented in Sacred Scripture, these brief daily meditations help us understand more clearly and deeply the meaning of suffering and death.

PRAYING WITH SCRIPTURE
IN THE HOLY LAND
Daily Mediations With the Risen Jesus 3.95

Msgr. David E. Rosage. Herein is offered a daily meeting with the Risen Jesus in those Holy Places which He sanctified by His human presence. Three hundred and sixty-five scripture texts are selected and blended with the pilgrimage experiences of the author, a retreat master, and well-known writer on prayer.

DISCERNMENT:
Seeking God in Every Situation   3.50

Rev. Chris Aridas. "Many Christians struggle with ways to seek, know and understand God's plan for their lives. This book is prayerful, refreshing and very practical for daily application. It is one to be read and used regularly, not just read" *(Ray Roh, O.S.B.).*

DISCOVERING
PATHWAYS TO PRAYER   3.95

Msgr. David E. Rosage. Following Jesus was never meant to be dull, or worse, just duty-filled. Those who would aspire to a life of prayer and those who have already begun, will find this book amazingly thorough in its scripture-punctuated approach.

"A simple but profound book which explains the many ways and forms of prayer by which the person hungering for closer union with God may find him" *(Emmanuel Spillane, O.C.S.O., Abbot, Our Lady of the Holy Trinity Abbey, Huntsville, Utah).*

MOURNING: THE HEALING JOURNEY 2.95

Rev. Kenneth J. Zanca. Comfort for those who have lost a loved one. Out of the grief suffered in the loss of both parents within two months, this young priest has written a sensitive, sympathetic yet humanly constructive book to help others who have lost loved ones. This is a book that might be given to the newly bereaved.

THE BORN-AGAIN CATHOLIC 4.95

Albert H. Boudreau. This book presents an authoritative imprimatur treatment of today's most interesting religious issue. The author, a Catholic layman, looks at Church tradition past and present and shows that the born-again experience is not only valid, but actually is Catholic Christianity at its best. The exciting experience is not only investigated, but the reader is guided into revitalizing his or her own Christian experience. The informal style, colorful personal experiences, and helpful diagrams make this book enjoyable and profitable reading.

WISDOM INSTRUCTS HER CHILDREN
The Power of the Spirit and the Word 3.95

John Randall, S.T.D. The author believes that now is God's time for "wisdom." Through the Holy Spirit, "power" has become much more accessible in the Church. Wisdom, however, lags behind and the result is imbalance and disarray. The Spirit is now seeking to pour forth a wisdom we never dreamed possible. This outpouring could lead us into a new age of Jesus Christ! This is a badly needed, most important book, not only for the Charismatic Renewal, but for the whole Church.

GRAINS OF WHEAT 3.50

Kelly B. Kelly. This little book of words received in prayer is filled with simple yet often profound leadings, exhortations and encouragement for daily living. Within the pages are insights to help one function as a Christian, day by day, minute by minute.

LIVING FLAME PRESS
Box 74, Locust Valley, N.Y. 11560

QUANTITY

_____ Manna in the Desert — 5.95

_____ Reconciliation — 5.95

_____ Post-Charismatic Experience — 4.50

_____ Finding Peace in Pain — 3.50

_____ Thirsting for God in Scripture — 2.95

_____ Praying with Mary — 3.50

_____ Journey into Contemplation — 3.95

_____ Spiritual Direction — 5.95

_____ Encountering the Lord in Daily Life — 4.50

_____ The Returning Sun — 2.50

_____ Bread for the Eating — 3.50

_____ Living Here and Hereafter — 2.95

_____ Praying With Scripture in the
         Holy Land — 3.95

_____ Discernment — 3.50

_____ Discovering Pathways to Prayer — 3.95

_____ Mourning: The Healing Journey — 2.95

_____ The Born Again Catholic — 4.95

_____ Wisdom Instructs Her Children — 3.95

_____ Grains of Wheat — 3.50

NAME _____

ADDRESS _____

CITY _____ STATE _____ ZIP _____

Kindly include $.70 postage and handling on orders up to $5; $1.00 on orders up to $10; more than $10 but less than $50, add 10% of total; over $50, add 8% of total. Canadian residents add 20% exchange rate, plus postage and handling. N.Y. State residents add 7% tax unless exempt.

119

128